D0051277

The Cold War
A Beginner's Guide

ONEWORLD BEGINNER'S GUIDES combine an original, inventive, and engaging approach with expert analysis on subjects ranging from art and history to religion and politics, and everything in between. Innovative and affordable, books in the series are perfect for anyone curious about the way the world works and the big ideas of our time.

anarchism	forensic science
artificial intelligence	french revolution
the beat generation	history of science
biodiversity	humanism
bioterror & biowarfare	islamic philosophy
the brain	journalism
the buddha	lacan
censorship	life in the universe
christianity	machiavelli
civil liberties	mafia & organized crime
classical music	marx
cloning	medieval philosophy
cold war	middle east
crimes against humanity	NATO
criminal psychology	oil
critical thinking	the palestine–israeli conflict
daoism	philosophy of mind
democracy	philosophy of religion
dyslexia	philosophy of science
energy	postmodernism
engineering	psychology
evolution	quantum physics
evolutionary psychology	the qur'an
existentialism	racism
fair trade	the small arms trade
feminism	sufism

The Cold War
A Beginner's Guide

Merrilyn Thomas

ONEWORLD
OXFORD

A Oneworld Paperback Original

Published by Oneworld Publications 2009

Copyright © Merrilyn Thomas 2009

The right of Merrilyn Thomas to be identified as
the Author of this work has been asserted by her in accordance with the
Copyright, Designs and Patents Act 1988

ISBN 978–1–85168–680–3

Typeset in Jayvee, Trivandrum, India
Cover design by Simon McFadden
Printed and bound in Great Britain
by Bell & Bain, Glasgow

Oneworld Publications
185 Banbury Road
Oxford OX2 7AR
England
www.oneworld-publications.com

Mixed Sources
Product group from well-managed
forests and other controlled sources
www.fsc.org   Cert no. TT-COC-002769
© 1996 Forest Stewardship Council

For Amos

Contents

Introduction

There probably never was a war more susceptible to myth making than the Cold War. Largely fought in secret by the intelligence services of the USA, the Soviet Union, Britain and the two Germanies, it was a battle for and of minds in which the main weapons were propaganda and deception. Certainly, transparency was not the aim of any of the main protagonists, nor was it their wish to leave a clear record for posterity. As a result, grasping the reality of the Cold War can be as tantalising as catching a sunbeam.

Manipulation of public attitudes was easier in the Cold War years than it is today. Compared to the world-weariness of the twenty-first century, it was a more trusting age. The aim of this book is to dispel some of the myths of the Cold War; to bring recently acquired knowledge to our understanding of events, and question perceptions which have, with the passage of time, tended to become certainties in the public consciousness. This book queries the validity of assumptions made in a world so divided that nearly everything was seen in black and white. As far as is possible, it peels back layers of deception and intrigue and moves beyond the mythology which has been so carefully constructed around the Cold War story. It examines events not only from the standpoint of the West but also from that of the Soviet Union and its allies. But there is a proviso. In the words of a British intelligence expert, governments offer only carefully packaged versions of the past.[1] It is unlikely that the parcel will ever be fully unwrapped.

Some of those who read this book will have lived through the Cold War and will have their own memories of events. I, myself, am a child of the Cold War, born in the year that Churchill added the term 'iron curtain' to the world's lexicon. Others, the generation born around the time when that most potent symbol of the conflict, the Berlin Wall, was demolished, will know it only second-hand. Most people, old or young, will have personal opinions about it. My random enquiries about the meaning of the term 'Cold War' have elicited a variety of responses. Some remember it as a superpower conflict between the Soviet Union and the USA. Some recall it as the period when Europe was divided. There are James Bond aficionados, too young to remember the events themselves, for whom, I am assured, the words 'Cold War' conjure up merely an image of a white Persian cat – the trademark of the villainous Dr Blofeld who plotted world domination.

In order to write about the Cold War it is necessary to define it. But this in itself is no easy task. For those who lived through it, it seemed real enough at the time. The world was rigidly divided along ideological lines for more than forty years. It was impossible to sit on the fence between communism and capital-ism, try though many smaller countries did. The fear of nuclear annihilation was a constant menacing cloud. But the more time passes, the more amorphous the idea of the Cold War becomes. With its ending, the era of ideological politics seemed to vanish into thin air, the world's leaders replaced by a new breed of managerial politicians, many of whom did not seem to believe in anything at all. How was it that the world could have fought so hard, for so long and so dangerously over what were merely philosophical ideals?

But was it an ideological conflict? The question is one that has, over the decades, aroused debate in historical circles. Indeed, some historians have taken the ideology out of the Cold War and argued that it was about international power politics and national self-interests. The schools of thought can be roughly divided into three groups. During the early years of the

Cold War, the orthodox view was that it was a struggle against Stalinist expansionism. During the middle years, the revisionists saw the conflict in terms of the USA's determination to impose itself and its economic system on the rest of the world. It was the post-revisionists during the latter years of the Cold War who cast the ideological factor to the winds. Since then, there has been a gradual return to stressing the importance of ideology.

This has partly come about because of the availability of new archive material from countries other than Western Europe or the USA, particularly the former Soviet bloc countries and Asia. This has added deeper understanding to the role that ideology played in dividing the world. It has shown more clearly how the main protagonists, particularly the two superpowers, judged other countries and regional conflicts by their ideological allegiances. This was the benchmark by which the Soviet Union and the USA determined which of the smaller nations were camp followers and which were not. Even when the political affiliation of another country was only skin deep, as was often the case in Africa or the Middle East, the perception from Washington or Moscow was of ideological commitment. There are several instances where US perception that an emerging African nation, for example, was ideologically sympathetic to communism, served to make it so.

The history of the Cold War for most people living in the West was, until the 1990s, the West's version of events. The availability of new archive material and a distance from events has enabled historians to redress a previously skewed picture. As a result, in recording this new history, some aspects of this book may be seen as unduly harsh on American and Western actions and motives. This is inevitable. The dissemination of information during the Cold War was not objective. It was aimed at winning a war. So, for example, the building of the Berlin Wall, still popularly portrayed as a heinous crime against humanity, was in reality a relief for the West because it stabilised an unstable situation. Or, nearer to our own time, the emergence in the 1970s of a strong new leader in Iraq called Saddam Hussein was greeted positively by both Britain and the USA. The Americans even sent a young emissary, by the name of Donald Rumsfeld, to have secret talks with him in 1983.

During the Cold War the media, from which most people derive their awareness of current events, was susceptible, both wittingly and unwittingly, to government propaganda. Latterly, the US government itself has set the record straight on some issues by releasing previously secret documents. Twenty years after the event, for example, it was revealed that Kennedy and Khrushchev had arranged a secret deal during the Cuban missile crisis. The drip of information about the Cold War will continue for many years to come. There will be more revelations, and perceptions will be modified again. The haphazard manner in which archive material becomes available means that evaluating the Cold War will remain a problem. A new document does not provide the final answer. It only adds a piece to the jigsaw.

All history is selective. This is particularly so with the Cold War because of its geographical extent and large time span. The tendency has been for historians to specialise in particular areas, either geographical or thematic. This book bucks that trend in that it ranges across the globe covering the period from the end of the Second World War to the quiet revolutions in Europe. In order to do this it has been necessary to select and to simplify the complex. The events described are a sample which illustrates the whole. They build up a picture. They contain and encapsulate the meaning of the Cold War. This book provides a starting point.

On a point of style, I have used 'Russia' and 'Russians' interchangeably with the 'Soviet Union' and 'Soviets'; likewise with America and the USA. All the countries on the eastern side of the Iron Curtain I have referred to as the Soviet bloc. America and her allies are 'the West'. This is a crude way to divide the world, necessitated by brevity. However, it should be noted that there were frequent differences of opinion between countries in the same power blocs. They did not necessarily act with one accord.

The chapter on Africa deals with sub-Saharan Africa, that area of the continent lying south of the Sahara Desert. North Africa is included in the chapter on the Middle East since the countries that make up this area – Morocco, Algeria, Tunisia, Libya and Egypt – are linked by history, religion, culture and ethnicity to the Middle East. Sub-Saharan Africa is the greater part of the continent including more than forty countries.

1

Communism and capitalism

Throughout the centuries the human condition has exercised the world's thinkers. Philosophers and philanthropists have sought to find ways of creating a better society. During the twentieth century, the ideal which dominated much of the world was of a society where all were free and equal, where no one was oppressed, and where everyone had everything they needed. It is possible to criticise this ideal as being hopelessly utopian but it does not appear to bear the hallmark of wickedness. Yet much of the last century was spent in a global struggle between those who purported to be the advocates of such an ideal and those who saw the doctrine behind it not only as a threat to existence but frequently as an evil. The utopian world was the world of communism; an integral part of the ideal was the annihilation of capitalism, the economic system which governs most of the globe, albeit somewhat shakily.

Communism, whether in theory or practice, dominates the history of the twentieth century. Its story is one not only of revolutions, wars and persecution but also of idealism and crusade. Human baseness and brutality mingle with heroism and sacrifice. During the 1930s, for example, thousands joined the International Brigades and went to their deaths in Spain in a civil war which was not their own because they believed in the cause. Thousands more perished during the same decade as a result of Stalin's purges.

Based on the nineteenth-century writings of the German philosopher Karl Marx, communism's first national power base was Russia. During the Russian Revolution of 1917, the monarchy was overthrown and a communist state established under Lenin's leadership. The USSR (Union of Soviet Socialist Republics) emerged from Imperial Russia in 1922. Russia's new revolutionary leaders faced hostility from Europe and the USA from the outset. They supported the counter-revolutionary forces, known as the White Russians. Winston Churchill in particular, at that time British Secretary of State for War, was vehemently opposed to Lenin and his comrades, known as the Bolsheviks, and advocated strong action against them. A Franco-British force landed in the Russian Arctic port of Murmansk in 1918 and occupied it for about two years. Civil war between the Whites and the Red Army lasted for nearly three years in the regions around Russia's borders. Britain recognised the Soviet regime in 1924; the USA did not do so until 1933. America warned that the Bolsheviks were a threat to social order in nearly every European country.

When, in 1918, the world's leaders met in Paris to draw up peace terms at the end of the First World War, it was the threat of Bolshevism spreading from the east rather than the fate of defeated Germany which was uppermost in many minds. Despite the fact that Russia had fought with Britain, France and the USA against Germany, Lenin and his comrades were excluded from the peace conference which devoted much of its time to devising ways either of destroying his revolution or preventing its spread.[1]

Three empires had collapsed by the end of the First World War – Russian, Turkish and Austro–Hungarian. With the map of Europe in tatters, one solution to the communist threat was to establish a *cordon sanitaire* of small independent nations in Eastern Europe, to isolate communism from capitalism. The new states were formed from the imperial remnants. But three decades later, as the Soviet army swept across Europe in the final months of the war against Hitler, these vulnerable nations fell under Russian influence. By 1945, they looked more like bridgeheads for communism than protection against the red peril. The Russian army stopped at the Elbe. The Iron Curtain descended roughly along that line.

As the century progressed, communism spread from Europe to all corners of the globe. China, the most populous nation in the world, became a communist state. Many other Asian nations followed suit. Latin American and African leaders declared themselves to be communist, although Lenin might not have recognised them as such. In addition, communist parties were established and sometimes flourished in almost every country in the world, including Western European countries. Yet, come the millennium, the communist experiment seemed to be over. During the 1990s, communist states collapsed like a pack of cards, a mere handful remaining to fly the ragged red flag by the end of the century.

Surely the big question about communism is what went wrong. Why did it fail? How was it that a humanistic doctrine became a Stalinist or Maoist tyranny?

Communism: the great fantasy

Many millions of words have been written in attempts to explain Marxism and communism since Marx first penned his brief *Manifesto of the Communist Party* in 1848.[2] Many millions have died fighting in the name of Marxism or communism. A significant number of these adherents have been killed, not by the opposition, but by others also claiming to be true Marxists or communists. So what is this creed which gripped and divided the world during the twentieth century and which remains, for some, a tyrannical abuse of humankind and, for others, the ultimate ideal?

There are two things that most commentators seem to have agreed upon over the decades: Marxism is not the same as communism, and Marxism itself is a matter of interpretation. 'There is scarcely any question relating to the interpretation of Marxism that is not a matter of dispute', according to one of the world's foremost experts on Marxism, the Polish émigré historian Leszek Kolakowski. His three-volume work on Marxism, in which he endeavoured to record the 'principal controversies', is regarded as one of the most influential books of the second half of the twentieth century.[3] His oft quoted conclusion was that Marxism was 'the greatest fantasy' of the century. 'It was a dream offering the prospect of a society of perfect unity, in which all human aspirations would be fulfilled and all values reconciled.'[4]

For those coming new to Marxism, the best introduction is a reading of the philosopher's own words on the subject contained in his brief *Manifesto*. First published in 1848, a time of revolution throughout Europe, it was a rallying cry to the dispossessed. Marx, the son of a prosperous middle class Jewish family, was banned from Germany and France because of his subversive activities and finally settled in London.[5] Much of what Marx wrote in his *Manifesto* has a contemporary ring. He foresaw the rise of the global economy. Indeed, for him it had already happened. The industrial revolution, the huge increase in trade resulting from colonisation and the resulting rise of the bourgeoisie had all served to create world markets and an international conformity. They had also created the proletariat and the bourgeoisie whose only bond, according to Marx, was the 'naked self-interest' of the bourgeoisie, owners of the capital with which the proletariat was exploited. But the bourgeoisie also sowed the seeds of its own destruction. Ultimately it would be destroyed by the working class that it had created.

The concept of inevitability in history is a crucial factor in Marxist theory. Marx claimed to have formulated a scientific theory by which man could know the future course of events. It was not possible to say, for example, when the revolution of the proletariat would happen, but it was possible to know that it inevitably would. This rigid belief in the eventual demise of capitalism made zealots of committed communists. Even in the direst of circumstances, the certainty of victory gave them strength. Communism, for some, resembled a religious faith with the added virtue that it could be scientifically proven. One theory to explain the collapse of communism is that, for a variety of reasons, this absolute belief weakened during the 1980s until there was no longer anything left to fight for.[6]

The distinguishing feature of communism, according to Marx, was the abolition of private property. Marx realised that this radical move was likely to meet stiff opposition, not just from the bourgeoisie at whom it was aimed but also from peasant farmers and small traders. He dealt with the problem in his *Manifesto* arguing that there was no need to destroy the latter type of property because it was in any case being destroyed by industrial development. 'Communism deprives no man of the power to appropriate the products of society; all that it does is to deprive him of the power to subjugate the labour of others by means of such appropriation', Marx claimed.[7]

Marxism provided the 'ideological tradition' on which communism was based.[8] Communism itself came in many forms. There was Marxism, Marxism-Leninism, Stalinism, and Maoism, to name but a few variations. Chinese Marxism, for example, wove Confucian philosophy into its tapestry during the twentieth century. In the twenty-first century it has also adopted its own version of capitalism. Latin American Marxists tended to focus on the economic exploitation of their countries by foreign powers rather than the home-grown bourgeoisie.

And then there is socialism. It is necessary, according to Marx, to go through a transitional stage between capitalism and communism and that stage is known as socialism. Communism is a higher form of socialism. During the transitional stage, the means of production are gathered into the hands of the state but the capitalist system continues. Some socialist parties never go beyond this stage. Many countries, as for example Sweden, practise a successful form of socialist welfare combined with capitalism. The use of the word 'socialist' to describe a political party or a government can be confusing as it can mean both one operating within the capitalist system or one which is on the road to communism. Many communist countries claimed to be 'socialist' and the word appeared in the official name of the Soviet Union.

Essentially, the Marxist proposition that the 'history of all hitherto existing society is the history of class struggle' and that the proletariat would inevitably take control throughout the world was central to communist dogma.[9] Once the proletariat had taken over, various measures would need to be introduced, Marx decreed. All 'instruments of production' would be placed in the hands of the state and all capital removed from the bourgeoisie. Initially the reorganisation of society would demand some 'despotic' measures, but once all production had been concentrated in the hands of the nation, public power would lose its political character. The state itself would wither away. For, as Marx put it: 'In place of the old bourgeois society, with its classes and class antagonisms, we shall have an association, in which the free development of each is the condition for the free development of all.'[10]

Marx's recipe for post-revolutionary society was followed on the whole by communist regimes. The problem was things did not follow the pattern that Marx had predicted. For example, those living under communism during the twentieth century found it more difficult to resolve the issue of private property than Marx had anticipated. Small farmers proved particularly resilient to the idea of losing their land. In many countries sweeping land reforms had to be watered down to prevent starvation. Even the East German leader, Walter Ulbricht, a committed communist and considered by many to be ultra

Stalinist, dared to introduce economic reforms in the 1960s which borrowed from capitalism. Faced with the all too visible economic miracle of West Germany, Ulbricht saw that it was necessary to make his workers' and peasants' state a more attractive place in which to live if his citizens were not to abandon the country for the bright lights of capitalism.[11] His heretical proposals, which spoke of profit and markets, were short lived, doomed to failure under pressure from the rigid orthodoxy of the Kremlin. Attempts by other Soviet bloc countries to liberalise their failing economies suffered similar fates.

Most importantly, the state did not wither away as Marx had predicted; it tended to become increasingly powerful and all-pervading. Kolakowski is not alone in asking how it was that this 'idea which began in Promethean humanism ... culminated in the monstrous tyranny of Stalin.' One of the answers is that Marx was wrong to think that once private property had been removed, 'human interest would cease to be in conflict'.

Other commentators have taken a more critical view of Marxism. The historian Richard Pipes, a US presidential adviser during the 1980s, sees no good in Marxism at all. His bald assessment is that 'Communism was not a good idea that went wrong; it was a bad idea'. Acquisitiveness is a powerful human characteristic. Communism could not refashion human nature. That is why it had to resort to coercion and violence in order to make people give up their private property. Communism, in Pipes' view, 'is a pseudoscience converted into a pseudoreligion and embodied in an inflexible political regime'.[12] The only solution to the world's problems is the free market; in other words, capitalism.

Capitalism: the consumers' creed

Capitalism is not, on the whole, a rallying cry. Passions can be raised by demands for 'freedom' or 'democracy'. Not many have taken to the streets on behalf of capitalism. And yet it is capitalism which has routed Marx's cry – 'Working men of all countries, unite!'[13]

Perhaps the simplest way of differentiating capitalism from communism is to ask the question: who or what rules? The short answer for communism is the proletariat; the short answer for capitalism is the market. One of the first to expound on the concept of the free market was the Scottish political economist Adam Smith in the eighteenth century. He was an advocate of free trade at a time when, in Britain, the movement of goods was strictly regulated. His study of the development of industry and commerce in Europe, *The Wealth of Nations*, is regarded as a classic. In it, Smith argued that, if people were set free to better themselves, it would in fact benefit the whole of society.

At the start of the twentieth century, the German political economist, Max Weber, attempted to capture the essence of capitalism in his book, *The Protestant Ethic and the Spirit of Capitalism*. Weber argued that the desire to accumulate wealth in order to acquire that which it can buy was an age old human ambition and not related to the concept of capitalism. What makes capitalism as practised in the West different is that the aim is to acquire wealth in order to invest it and in turn produce more wealth. This goal has its roots in the Protestant faith, Weber said. Those who use their money to buy fast cars and lavish lifestyles would not, according to Weber, be capitalists. Those who invest their money to expand their businesses, would be. In his words:

> Unlimited greed for gain is not in the least identical with capitalism, and is still less its spirit. Capitalism *may* even be identical with the restraint, or at least a rational tempering, of this irrational impulse. But capitalism is identical with the pursuit of profit, and forever *renewed* profit, by means of

continuous, rational, capitalistic enterprise. For it must be so: in a wholly capitalistic order of society, an individual capitalistic enterprise which did not take advantage of its opportunities for profit-making would be doomed to extinction.[14]

About forty years later, an Austrian political scientist, Joseph Schumpeter, attempted to tackle the vexed question of capitalism. His study, *Capitalism, Socialism and Democracy*, which examined the relationship between the political system of democracy and the economic systems of socialism and capitalism, opened up a new debate.[15] Writing during the Second World War and with the memory of the Great Depression still strong, Schumpeter argued that socialism and democracy were not incompatible and that capitalism would eventually give way to socialism.

Looked at from the perspective of the twenty-first century, Schumpeter seems to have been wrong. With the ending of the Cold War, not only was capitalism victorious but also a consensus was established that capitalism and democracy are inextricably linked. According to a study conducted in the early part of the 1990s, in which a number of leading scholars re-examined Schumpeter's arguments, this link was forged at the end of the Cold War.[16] The contributors to the study were asked to examine the validity of the perception that democracy can flourish only in a market economy. Interestingly, all of them, whether champions of capitalism or socialism, endorsed a mixed economy as the ideal though they differed on the emphasis that should be placed on state intervention and the market.

More recently, the American political economist, Jeffry Frieden, has tried to answer the question of whether global capitalism will last. Globalisation, the economic system to which Marx referred in his *Manifesto*, is now, according to Frieden, taken for granted. Many people 'regard it as the natural state of things, and expect that it will last for ever'.[17] But, says Frieden, its base is as fragile as it was in the early twentieth century when it was swept away by the First World War, only to re-emerge at the end of the Cold War. Its survival, according to Frieden, depends on an acceptance by governments of social obligation. There is no moral yardstick with which to measure the suffering of a worker who loses his job in one part of the world against the benefits to another worker thousands of miles away whose job depends on globalisation, he writes. The success of global capitalism will depend on the ability of governments to co-exist with policies committed to social advance.[18]

Some scholars predicted a crisis in capitalism, pointing out that the Protestant ethos, as referred to by Weber, has been lost. According to the American political theorist, Benjamin Barber, capitalism's success is also its downfall. Too many goods are now chasing too few needs and so needs have to be manufactured.[19] Shopping has become an addiction, consumerism 'a surrogate for living'.[20] 'Global inequality means that while the wealthy have too few needs, the needy have too little wealth. Capitalism is stymied, courting long-term disaster.' Barber asks the question: 'How is it that when we see politics permeate every life sector we call it totalitarianism and when we see religion everywhere we call it theocracy, but when commerce dominates everything we call it liberty?'[21] In order to survive, says Barber, capitalism will have to respond to real needs again instead of fabricating synthetic ones, or else it will consume itself – thus raising the question of whether Marx's prophecy that capitalism contains the seeds of its own destruction could even yet prove to be true. The 'credit crunch' of 2008 and 2009 has seen capitalism struggling for survival.

There was a logical inevitability to the conflict between capitalism and communism. Although there was a period during the late 1960s and 1970s when co-existence was attempted, the two systems could not exist side by side indefinitely. The problem was not only that, ideologically, the success of one entailed the death of the other; it was also that both systems demanded continuous expansion at the expense of the other. Growth is essential for capitalism in order to obtain return on investment. World domination was inherent within communism. Like two swelling toads in a confined space, one system was doomed to crush the other or both would explode.

By the end of the twentieth century, it appeared that capitalism had triumphed. There was little to stand in its way as the former communist world scrambled to board the capitalist boat. But the free rein handed to capitalism with the demise of communism has resulted in a global crisis. The events of the first decade of the twenty-first century have demonstrated that there are unforeseen dangers inherent in the dominance of a global economic system unconstrained by alternative forces.

2
Propaganda, plots and bombs

The conflict between communism and capitalism culminated in the Cold War. For more than four decades the world was dangerously divided along an ideological fault line. It was a largely secret war, the greater part being fought by the intelligence agencies of the main protagonists. What people were able to observe was only the tip of the iceberg. A few years after the Cold War had come to an end in Europe, a leading American historian famously wrote a book prematurely entitled *We Now Know: Rethinking Cold War History*. Its author, John Lewis Gaddis, has since qualified that statement. What we know now is simply more than we did.[1] Intelligence expert Richard J. Aldrich has detailed our lack of accurate information about the Cold War in a book about what he calls 'the hidden hand'. This, he says, is the missing dimension of Cold War history, the work of the intelligence agencies. We do not yet know the full story of the Cold War and we may never know, he writes. What we can be certain of is that intelligence activity is 'fundamental to any understanding of the Cold War ... [it] was fought, above all, by the intelligence services'.[2]

It is this fact that makes the Cold War so unlike other major conflicts which have occurred throughout the centuries. Although intelligence services have almost always played a part in wars, the fact remains that conflicts have largely been determined by military operations. These are difficult to hide from public view even though attempts may be made to distort the outcomes. But the Cold War was not fought with set piece battles. Although it rapidly spilled over from its European origins to encompass Asia, Africa, the Middle East and Latin America, most countries did not experience warfare during the Cold War. Even in those countries which were ravaged by conventional battles, such as Korea, Vietnam and Afghanistan, the conflict was primarily a civil war which was appropriated by one or other of the two power blocs thus enabling the Cold War to be fought by proxy.

The tools of intelligence agencies are many and varied. They include deception, sabotage, espionage, subversion, secret propaganda and, on occasion, political assassination. This chapter offers up merely the flavour of the clandestine Cold War. It aims to provide an understanding of the context in which events took place, an antidote to the official versions preferred by governments. Western governments, for example, have tended to lead their citizens to believe that the nefarious secret deeds of the Cold War emanated from 'the other side', that the West's intelligence role was largely defensive rather than offensive. In reality, both sides were actively engaged in the whole range of intelligence activities over several decades. The Russians, for example, were as concerned about Western infiltration as the West was about communist infiltration. Subversive plots were dreamt up in London and Washington as well as Moscow. But the history of the Cold War suffers from a problem common to the histories of most conflicts in that it is the victor's version which becomes the norm.

The area of intelligence activity which probably sits highest in the public consciousness is that of espionage, largely because this most secret of occupations was also, when spies were caught, the most public. There were many spy scandals throughout the Cold War. Examples include the Cambridge spies, chief among them Kim Philby, Guy Burgess and Donald Maclean.[3] The East German secret service managed to place a spy in the inner office of the West German Chancellor, Willy Brandt. Günter Guillaume spent several years feeding information to the Stasi before being arrested in 1974.[4] The traffic was two-way. In 1967 alone, the KGB claims to have identified more than 270 foreigners in Russia with links to Western intelligence services and uncovered twenty-two double agents.[5]

Spies capture the public imagination. But the bulk of intelligence activity during the Cold War was focused on 'the struggle for the minds of men',[6] otherwise known as psychological warfare – the art of influencing attitudes, not only of the enemy but also of non-aligned and domestic audiences. It ranges from the use of propaganda radio stations to the manipulation of the news media, the creation of resistance groups and a whole range of covert and often murky operations.[7]

The common characteristic of Cold War psychological warfare was its 'plausible deniability'. These words first occurred in an American National Security Council statement in 1948, which ruled that covert operations must be 'planned and executed so that any US Government responsibility for them is not evident to unauthorised persons and that if uncovered the US Government can plausibly disclaim any responsibility'.[8] The Labour Cabinet member and Second World War psychological warrior Richard Crossman put it more succinctly: 'The way to carry out good propaganda is never to appear to be carrying it out at all.'[9]

Although the main protagonists in the Cold War, both militarily and in the field of intelligence, were the Soviet Union and the USA, Britain played a role greater than her international status warranted when it came to the clandestine world. This was partly because of the close connections between the US and British intelligence agencies which had been established during the Second World War. Many Americans learned their trade from the British. In addition, British colonial history provided her with a wealth of worldwide clandestine networks and installations which, despite the decline of empire, continued to prove invaluable.

The other country which punched above its weight was the German Democratic Republic (GDR), which rapidly established an impressive intelligence service during the 1950s. The Stasi, like the KGB, was responsible for both domestic and foreign intelligence activities. The great advantage for the East Germans in the field of overseas operations was the relative ease with which it could infiltrate its home-grown agents into the West German political establishment. With no language or cultural differences to overcome, an East German agent could easily pass himself off as a West German.

The bulk of clandestine activity was low key. The intelligence services made use of people who had genuine reasons to be in a particular country – businessmen, journalists, religious leaders, academics – and used them to provide information and contacts. Foreign correspondents were ideally placed. The CIA, for example, is reported to have had more than 400 American journalists on its books during the first thirty years of the Cold War. Usually with the knowledge and agreement of their publishers, they provided the CIA with information and undercover services. While not being spies themselves, they helped the CIA to recruit spies by acting as go-betweens. Sometimes a publisher provided journalistic cover for official CIA operatives. Information about the CIA's journalistic network was revealed by the Church Committee in 1975 and, subsequently, in greater detail by *Washington Post* journalist, Carl Bernstein.[10]

The British conducted their own anti-communist propaganda operations through a secret organisation known innocuously as the Information Research Department (IRD), established in 1948 as a unit within the Foreign Office. The Foreign Secretary, Ernest Bevin, a member of the recently elected socialist government, had taken some persuading of the need for such an organisation. He preferred to promote the

The **Church Committee** was set up in 1975 in order to investigate American covert operations and was named after its chairman, Senator Frank Church. Its full title was the Senate Select Committee to Study Governmental Operations with Respect to Intelligence Activities. The Watergate Affair and revelations about other US covert operations, assassination attempts and espionage activities persuaded the US Senate that it had been too lax in carrying out its duty of oversight over the administration. It concluded that clandestine operations needed to be carried out under the rule of law and proper safeguards should be in place to ensure that this was so. In effect, the committee conducted a detailed public appraisal of US intelligence agencies. The Church Committee issued fourteen reports in 1975 and 1976, most of which are now available to the public. They can be read on the website of the Assassination Archives and Research Center (AARC) at http://www.aarclibrary.org/publib/church/ reports/contents.htm

positive aspects of the British attitude rather than aggressively denounce communism. He also faced two other problems. A significant proportion of the British public still sympathised with the Russians as a result of wartime co-operation; and he risked a split in the Labour Party. A number of socialist MPs deplored what they called the 'anti-red virus'. They, and indeed Bevin, wanted to see Britain taking a line between the Soviet Union and the USA. 'You have got two great imperialisms [Soviet and American] without, I am afraid, quite all the experience that this stupid old country has got', Bevin told the press in 1946.[11] He had argued that it was up to the British government as European social democrats and not the USA to give a lead in the spiritual, moral and political sphere.

The IRD produced briefing papers on subjects such as 'Forced Labour in the USSR', and 'Training the Young for Stalin', which were disseminated around the world. At home the IRD used the press and the BBC as outlets for its propaganda efforts. Abroad, it targeted journalists, diplomats and politicians through its embassies. The cardinal rule was that, in order to make it believable, information coming from the IRD should not be identified as such. It is claimed that by 1977, when the IRD was closed, it had more than 100 British journalists from nearly every national newspaper on its books who unwittingly used IRD material.[12]

American intelligence agencies were particularly active in attempting to undermine Soviet bloc countries during the early Cold War years. The aim was to destabilise countries such as Poland and the GDR by encouraging resistance movements. Washington told those in the field that:

> overt measures should be used only to nourish the spirit of resistance, not to advocate openly specific acts of resistance. The reasons for these limitations ... are: 1) that we do not want to risk precipitating prematurely a mass, open rebellion or, if one does take place prematurely, to incur blame for the consequences; and 2) that we do not want to throw doubt on the spontaneous nature of the resistance.[13]

Intelligence agencies did not confine themselves to operations directed at the enemy. Very often they kept a wary eye on their own allies, sometimes trying to influence their decision-making processes. Both the IRD and the CIA secretly intervened in the French and Italian election campaigns during 1948, fearing communist successes. But the British and Americans were also frequently at odds over Cold War policy. The British thought the Americans were too gung-ho; that their attempts to subvert the Soviet bloc and mastermind revolts could lead to a third world war. The British 'focused on containing the possibility of war, more than on containing communism. In practice that meant containing Washington'.[14] Another bone of contention was the future political direction of Western Europe. The USA favoured a federal Europe in its own image as a bulwark against communism. Britain did not. During the 1950s, the CIA worked to undermine British policy. It actively encouraged the development of a federal Europe by secretly pouring money into the European Movement, an organisation set up to promote European union and institutions such as the Council of Europe.[15]

On the other side of the Iron Curtain, the Russians created a propaganda organisation known as the Cominform in 1947, partly in an attempt to counter the American Marshall Aid programme in Europe and partly to encourage the spread of communism. It was short lived, being shut down by Khrushchev in 1956 as a gesture towards a more co-operative era.

The activities of intelligence agencies were not confined to manipulation and subversion. Assassination was also a tool of the trade. The Church Committee investigated a number of alleged CIA plots to murder foreign leaders. These included Patrice Lumumba of the Congo, Fidel Castro of Cuba, Rafael Trujillo of the Dominican Republic, Ngo Dinh Diem of Vietnam and Rene Schneider of Chile. It found that the CIA had initiated plots to kill Lumumba and Castro but that the evidence was inconclusive in the other cases. Assassination was also an 'integral part of Stalin's foreign policy'.[16] Documents show that he drew up plans to assassinate the independently minded President of Yugoslavia, Josip Tito. Khrushchev and his successors used assassination as a weapon against defectors.

Despite continuing secrecy, Gaddis was right to say that we now know much more about the Cold War. A huge number of books and articles have been published on the conflict since the 1990s. Nevertheless our knowledge remains a drop in the ocean. The majority of writers will at some point refer to the 'new archival sources' on which their books are based. But, while it is true that, across the globe, historians are now delving into documents which would have remained closed had the Cold War not ended, the one area where this does not hold true is intelligence. The archives of intelligence agencies, with some exceptions, remain closed. Even when information is released, it is highly selective and may distort rather than clarify. There is, according to Aldrich, no 'historical free lunch'. Governments press on historians and journalists what they want them to know. Indeed, Aldrich suggests that governments may attempt deliberately to mislead. He cites the fact that US officials proposed releasing material relating to the Kennedy assassination as a distraction from other areas where the probing of researchers would be less welcome.[17]

Secret intelligence agencies like to keep their activities secret even after the event. This is true of both the Soviet KGB and the British MI6. Very little has been released from the KGB archive. Most researchers have to rely on second-hand information from former KGB officers. One major exception relates to the former KGB officer Vasili Mitrokhin. Over many years, he secretly squirrelled away thousands of KGB files. When he defected to Britain in 1992, these files were smuggled out of Russia and, in co-operation with the British intelligence expert Christopher Andrew, some of the contents were published in two books.[18]

In Britain, despite the fact that the Secret Intelligence Service (SIS), better known as MI6, was formed in 1909, its very existence was not officially admitted until 1992. The same is true of its sister organisation MI5. The archives of MI6 are closed. MI5 has released several hundred files to the National Archives but only covering the period up to the late 1950s. Both organisations are engaged in preparing official histories.

In contrast to British and Russian secrecy, the Americans are almost embarrassingly candid about their activities. The CIA was founded in 1947 and the following year a unit was created within it responsible for planning and conducting covert operations in peacetime. Covert operations were defined as being:

propaganda; economic warfare; preventive direct action, including sabotage, anti-sabotage, demolition, and evacuation measures; subversion against hostile states, including assistance to underground resistance movements, guerrillas and refugee liberation groups.[19]

Thousands of CIA documents and reports can be accessed online. In addition, US institutions such as the Cold War International History Project and the National Security Archive keep up a steady flow of documents and publications.[20] The quantity of previously classified US documents released increased substantially after President Clinton, in 1995, ordered government agencies to release to the public material more than twenty-five years old. Nevertheless, these documents only scratch the surface.

One way of unearthing information about the activities of agencies with closed archives is through the archives of their foreign counterparts. It is, for example, possible to find references to the activities of MI5 and MI6 within the CIA's online archive.[21] Another rich seam to mine is the East German Stasi archive. This, along with GDR government archives, was opened to researchers following the collapse of the Berlin Wall and reunification in 1990. Although the files of the department dealing with foreign intelligence activities mysteriously vanished during the upheavals of the time, resurfacing in the possession of the CIA, they have since been returned and are open to researchers on a restricted basis. References to the activities of foreign intelligence agencies can be found within these files.

The main players in the Cold War had a huge amount of clandestine expertise on which to draw. Britain, America and Russia did not come as novices to the fields of psychological warfare and covert operations. The Second World War had provided them with an excellent training ground. Both Britain and America had used covert and overt propaganda methods to

One of the strangest stories to emerge from the last few days of the Cold War concerns the manner in which some of the files belonging to the Stasi were spirited away in the chaos surrounding the fall of the Berlin Wall only to resurface in America in the hands of the CIA. Most of the information related to the Stasi's activities in the West. The danger was that these files could have blown the cover of people and organisations operating in the West on behalf of intelligence services. There are various stories about how this material came to be in the hands of the CIA. Some say that when a mob of East Germans attacked and ransacked the Stasi HQ, the CIA grabbed the opportunity by joining in and making off with it. It has also been suggested that they may have been working with the KGB, both organisations sharing the common concern that the archive should not fall into other hands. Others say the files were sold to the CIA by a former Stasi agent. But the explanation of how Stasi files found their way to Washington remains speculation – a mystery which demonstrates how the secret Cold War continues to throw up the dark and unexpected. Lengthy negotiations between the government of the new united Germany and Washington resulted in the data relating to Germany being returned to Berlin in 2003, this process being known as Operation Rosewood.

fight the Germans. They had set up organisations to carry out this secret work – the Political Warfare Executive (PWE) and the Special Operations Executive (SOE) in Britain and the Office of Strategic Services (OSS) in America. In the early years of the Cold War, the new secret agencies drew on this legacy.

The Russians, for their part, have a long history of covert operations. During the first half of the twentieth century, communism had thrived on intrigue and secrecy. In 1919, for example, the Russians had set up an organisation known as the Comintern with the object of spreading the communist revolution to other countries by subversive means. The Russians had established a number of intelligence networks throughout the world during the Second World War, most of which survived. Although intelligence activities had initially been targeted on Europe and Asia, the number of Soviet agents in the USA was greatly increased once Stalin and Roosevelt became wartime allies. Stalin distrusted his new friends, fearing they might make a separate peace agreement with Hitler and then wage a united war against the Soviet Union.[22] During the 1950s, these intelligence networks were eventually reformed into the KGB, which became responsible for foreign and domestic intelligence activities.

There were two reasons why intelligence activities were of such importance during the Cold War. One was because this was an ideological conflict. Winning it entailed changing attitudes, persuading the other side and the non-aligned that one ideology or system was preferable to another. In such a struggle, propaganda is probably the most effective weapon. The other reason was the existence of nuclear weapons. On 6 August 1945, the Americans dropped an atomic bomb on the Japanese city of Hiroshima, bringing the Second World War to a close and marking the start of the nuclear age. The significance of the destruction of Hiroshima for the Cold War was that the major participants were always constrained by the knowledge that weapons existed powerful enough to destroy people by the million. The British Prime Minister Clement Attlee remarked only days after Hiroshima that 'even the modern conception of war to which in my lifetime we have become accustomed is now completely out of date ... this invention has made it essential to end wars ... the whole conception of war [must be] banished from people's minds and from the calculations of government'.[23] The possessors of nuclear weapons had to find ways of fighting the Cold War without, on the whole, resorting to armed conflict or risk destroying the world they sought to control.

Initially there was a weapons imbalance. The USA was the only country with an atomic bomb in 1945. But the Soviet

Union, Britain and France rapidly closed the gap. The Russians detonated their first atomic bomb in 1949. A few months later President Truman announced that the USA would develop the much more powerful hydrogen bomb. The British tested their first atomic bomb in 1952, a month before the first test of the American hydrogen bomb. The Russians were only a few months behind. By 1953, the participants in the arms race were into their second lap. France joined the nuclear club in 1960.

The question that continues to be debated is the extent to which nuclear weapons prevented a major military conflict during the Cold War. Did their very existence preserve stability and peace? Or did the existence of these weapons of mass destruction delay the end of the Cold War?[24] Certainly, nuclear weapons became an important part of the international political equation. They may not have been used to kill but they were used to deter, to persuade, to bargain with, to protect, and to bring pressure to bear.

The history of the Cold War is littered with acronyms and abbreviations that tell the story of the world's attempts both to control the nuclear threat and to use it. To name but a few: SALT (Strategic Arms Limitation Talks between the USA and the Soviet Union in 1969 and 1972); START (Strategic Arms Reduction Talks in 1988); MAD (Mutual Assured Destruction, a strategy whereby the Kennedy administration encouraged a so-called second strike capability thus ensuring that a first strike did not take place); ABM (Anti-Ballistic Missile which would protect against a missile strike. Some argued against its development because it would negate MAD); SIOP (Single Integrated Operational Plan, the Nixon administration nuclear war plan); and SDI (Strategic Defense Initiative, the Reagan administration's plan to use space-based weapons systems).[25]

Nuclear weapons were the constant background to the Cold War. Their existence transformed minor skirmishes or disagreements into potential Armageddons. It was that knowledge that ratcheted up the tensions surrounding political and military actions which might otherwise have been inconsequential, thus creating the period of heightened hostilities we call the Cold War.

Just how clandestine operations and military power coalesced in the decades after 1945 to influence and in some ways create and extend the Cold War will be described in the following chapters. But first an answer needs to be sought as to how and why the conflict began. Why was it that only months after Britain, the USA and the Soviet Union, together with their allies, had emerged victorious from the Second World War, the world was again divided by an even greater and more dangerous conflict?

3

The freeze: from the Second World War to the division of Europe

As the citizens of Europe who had survived the carnage of the Second World War drew breath and prayed for a better life, the victorious political leaders began their journey into the new conflict which was to last for the next forty-five years. Unbeknown to the populace in general, the seeds of the Cold War had been germinating long before Hitler's defeat. There were several occasions during the latter months of the war against Germany which, with hindsight and access to archives, show that the Cold War was being fought simultaneously with the battle against Hitler.[1] Peace was an illusion. Tensions rose as the two sides, communist and capitalist, became ever more entrenched. The gap widened as fear of the other side increased. Attitudes became increasingly rigid; and both sides, through propaganda, encouraged these attitudes to intensify at home in order to win popular support for their policies. Within a few short years, the wartime allies became implacable foes.

All was harmonious on the surface, however, when the three leaders met at Potsdam in July 1945 to flesh out some of the Yalta agreements. Chief among the items on the agenda was the future of Germany. *The Times* noted in November 1945, with admirable prescience, that:

> It is in Germany that dissensions between the major Powers,
> whatever the ostensible origin of the contention, will make
> themselves felt, if not initially, then ultimately with the most
> serious consequences. Those who encourage or perpetuate
> these dissensions take a grave responsibility for the results which
> are likely to ensue in Germany and in Europe.

It had already been decided at Yalta that for practical purposes Germany would be divided into zones to be administered by the victors. But the stated intention was that this was a temporary measure. It had been agreed that in the foreseeable future Germany would be reunited. Within four years, however, Germany had been transformed into two separate states, West Germany and the GDR. The division of Germany symbolised the division of the world and the conflict which became the Cold War. Whose fault was it that an iron curtain was created across Europe? Which side was to blame: the Russians or the Americans?

The Allies were falling out almost before the ink was dry on the Potsdam agreement. In October 1945, the first meeting of foreign ministers in London set up to provide a forum for discussion on Germany broke down. Although later the West claimed that the division of Germany had been forced upon it by Stalin, research now suggests that essentially the division of Germany was more favoured by the USA and Britain than the Soviet Union. Western talk of a unified Germany was merely a 'figleaf'.[2] A British government top secret report confessed some years later that: 'Though we cannot admit it publicly, both sides would gain by avoiding the reunification of Germany.'[3] Stalin might have accepted a neutral demilitarised Germany. What he would not accept was a Germany drawn into the economic and military alliance of the West. But a strong anti-communist West Germany rapidly became a Western priority with the aim being to shift the blame for the division. In 1946, a British diplomat was quoted as saying that 'we have to make the Russians appear to the German public as the saboteurs of German unity'.[4]

The speed with which Europe was divided is remarkable. By March 1946, less than a year after Potsdam, Churchill was in the USA making his famous speech in which he declared that:

> From Stettin in the Baltic to Trieste in the Adriatic an iron curtain has descended across the Continent. Behind that line lie all the capitals of the ancient states of Central and Eastern Europe. Warsaw, Berlin, Prague, Vienna, Budapest, Belgrade, Bucharest and Sofia, all these famous cities and the populations around them lie in what I must call the Soviet sphere, and all are subject in one form or another, not only to Soviet influence but to a very high and, in some cases, increasing measure of control from Moscow.[5]

He went on to warn that communist parties or fifth columns prepared to co-operate with the enemy were increasingly active throughout the world and should be viewed as 'a growing challenge and peril to Christian civilization'. The view from Moscow was that communism flourished because it was ordinary people on the political left who had fought most strongly against fascism. Now they were being attacked again, this time by the capitalist West, which was in league with former fascists. For Stalin, Churchill's speech further demonstrated the threat that the West presented to the Soviet Union and its allies. Both sides distrusted and feared the other.

One of the details that had to be resolved in the post-Second World War chaos was the question of Berlin. As the capital of defeated Germany, the city had symbolic significance. The problem was that it lay entirely within the Soviet zone of occupation.

The decision was taken to divide it into four sectors, each sector to be occupied by one of the three wartime allies plus

By the early months of 1945 the war was all but won. The Red Army was advancing across Poland towards Berlin and British and American troops, after setbacks on the Rhine, were moving towards the German capital from the west. It seemed as though the race for Berlin was on. In the event, the American Supreme Allied Commander in Europe, General Dwight Eisenhower, decided to halt the Western advance at the Elbe about 50 miles from Berlin and focus on residual German opposition in the south. During the Cold War that followed, there were many critics of his decision. Berlin was taken and occupied by the Red Army in April 1945, and it appeared that Eisenhower had handed the city to the Russians on a plate. He had also annoyed the British who had realised that the city was a vitally significant victory trophy and had urged that they and the Americans should be allowed to press on to Berlin. Eisenhower, failing to foresee the coming conflict with the Russians, judged that for military reasons his army should focus on the south. Indeed he was also anxious to avoid any accidental conflict with his eastern ally, which could have happened if both armies had continued to advance and had met head on in Berlin. Stalin, on the other hand, knew full well the political importance of capturing Berlin. Not only did he recognise that the taking of the capital was the major symbolic act which would demonstrate that Hitler had been defeated; he was also distrustful of his Western allies. He suspected that the Germans were secretly aiding the Western advance, preferring Berlin to be taken by British and American troops rather than the feared Red Army. It is, however, debatable whether Eisenhower's decision had much impact on future events in the long run since it had already been decided at Yalta that Berlin would fall within the Soviet area of occupation.

France, the whole to be administered jointly. Berlin was to be a separate entity, not a part of any of the German zones. But because of its geographical position and the fact that it could only be accessed from the west by crossing the Soviet zone, the city was a thorn in the side of the Western allies throughout the Cold War. It became a weapon which Moscow could use to increase pressure when required for both domestic and international purposes. For the Russians, West Berlin was an anomaly; a 'bone stuck in our throat' according to Khrushchev who had a talent for a colourful phrase. Berlin became a constant source of tension. The West's commitment to maintaining its presence there meant that the status of Berlin could influence events on the other side of the world. The city was always part of the equation. The fear was always there; what about Berlin?

Another unresolved Second World War problem which added to Cold War tensions was that the former allies never concluded a peace treaty with the defeated Germany. As time went by, Russia frequently threatened to conclude its own peace treaty with the GDR. This would have been an act of enormous political significance. Neither Britain nor America was prepared to recognise the existence of the GDR until well into the 1970s. In addition, control of access to West Berlin would have passed from the Russians to the GDR once it ceased to be an occupied country. Giving the GDR leader this power was anathema to the West, which continued to see Ulbricht as a hardline Stalinist long after Stalin was dead – an impression encouraged by the Russians when they felt like presenting themselves as a better option than Ulbricht. A further complication was that Ulbricht nursed the fear that the Russians might one day abandon the GDR for political gains elsewhere. One historian has described the East German state as 'Stalin's unwanted child'.[6] Ulbricht therefore had an interest in increasing East–West tensions to ensure that the Russians remained tied to their German state. Whether anyone or any country really wanted a united Germany at any point during the Cold War is a moot point, despite the fact that at various times and for various political reasons both East and West professed that they did.

The Americans call the tune

By 1947, any doubts about US intentions towards the Soviet Union and communism had been removed. The USA committed itself to confronting the perceived communist threat. The term used to describe this policy was 'containment'. The manner in which this policy was to be carried out was encapsulated within the Truman Doctrine and followed up with concrete action in the Marshall Plan. Essentially, America would not use its military might to stop the spread of communism; it would use its economic power instead. The USA pledged itself to providing huge amounts of money to an exhausted Europe decimated by war so that it could build up its economy again. Truman told the American people:

> I believe that it must be the policy of the United States to support free peoples who are resisting attempted subjugation by armed minorities or by outside pressures. I believe that we must assist free peoples to work out their own destinies in their own way. I believe that our help should be primarily through economic and financial aid which is essential to economic stability and orderly political processes ... The seeds of totalitarian regimes are nurtured by misery and want. They spread and grow in the evil soil of poverty and strife. They reach their full growth when the hope of a people for a better life has died. We must keep that hope alive.[7]

The Marshall Plan, drawn up in June 1947, offered US financial aid to European countries on condition that these countries traded with America. Europe was provided with the dollars it needed in order to buy goods from the USA. Thus the economies of both areas were stimulated. The Soviet Union and East European countries were not excluded from this deal, but it was deliberately couched in terms that Stalin could not accept. Stalin also put pressure on other countries in the Eastern bloc to refuse American aid. He perceived the Marshall Plan as being directed against the Soviet Union, as a means by which the USA would control Europe and shape it in its own image. He reacted accordingly, tightening the Soviet Union's hold on its satellite states to ensure that they could not be enticed away from the communist fold by American dollars. Thus the Marshall Plan solidified the Cold War division of Europe.

By 1950, the former allies had parted company to such an extent that both sides claimed that they faced the threat of world domination by the other. The Americans argued that they needed to increase military and economic strength in order to counter Soviet aggression. The National Security Council drew up a policy document, famously known as NSC 68, which talked in apocalyptic terms and concluded that 'the gravest threat to the security of the United States within the foreseeable future stems from the hostile designs and formidable power of the

A top secret directive from the US National Security Council with the uninspiring title of **NSC 68** is regarded as being one of the most significant policy statements of the Cold War because it provided the USA with the *raison d'être* it needed to use force against communism. It accepted that America had the right or, as seen by some, the duty, to impose its order on the whole of the world. NSC 68 was the basis for US foreign and military policy from 1950 onwards and was drawn up shortly before US troops landed in South Korea. It stated that there was a basic incompatibility between communism and the Western world and that the USA should be prepared to use force if necessary to defend its principles of democratic freedom. Global and national security were inseparable. It was first referred to by *The Times* in 1964 when its existence became common knowledge following the death of General Douglas MacArthur and the release of his posthumous papers. He had been sacked by Truman when he argued in favour of using nuclear weapons in Korea.

USSR, and from the nature of the Soviet system'. The survival of the 'free world' was at stake, it said. The American aim was to reduce Russian power and influence by any means short of war. Containment had moved on to 'rollback'.

Soviet archives opened since the Cold War ended indicate that Washington knowingly exaggerated the Russian threat. Stalin was not planning to attack Western Europe if only for the pragmatic reason that his country was too weak to do so, both economically and militarily. His aim was to maintain the Soviet sphere of influence in Eastern Europe and promote the communist parties of Western Europe. Finland is an interesting case in point. Sharing a border with the Soviet Union, it seemed to be in a vulnerable position. Nevertheless it maintained its independence and its democratic institutions. Successive Finnish presidents succeeded in holding a neutral line. Could 'Finlandisation', the term coined to describe this delicate balancing act, have worked elsewhere? Stalin's attitude to Finland suggests that the West's fears of communist domination were more imagined than real.

Nevertheless, anti-communist hysteria gripped the USA. From across the Atlantic, in the post-war years, it looked as though European nations were falling like ninepins. Left-wing governments had been established in Bulgaria and Romania in 1945; Tito had taken control in Yugoslavia (although he proved to be a troublesome ally for the Kremlin); communists had taken over in Czechoslovakia in 1948; civil war between communists and monarchists had raged in Greece between 1946 and 1947 and had been a motivating factor behind the Truman Doctrine; Poland became a communist state in 1948; Hungary became a People's Republic in 1949; Moscow's German protégé Ulbricht returned to Berlin in 1945 and rapidly took control of the eastern zone of Germany. Even supposedly friendly states seemed to be wavering. Communist parties were strong in both France and Italy. In 1948, the Americans used both covert operations and economic power in order to ensure that the Christian Democrats defeated the communist party in the Italian general election. In France, the approach was more subtle with the USA supporting the moderate socialist party in order to split and thereby weaken the left. Even the British looked wobbly, electing a socialist government in 1945. The suggestion that too much socialism might hinder American aid to Britain at a time of great need helped to dampen socialist rhetoric in Britain in the early post-war years.[8]

The rest of the world was not looking too good either, as seen from Washington. There was a civil war in China where Mao Zedong's communist supporters were challenging the government and there was unrest in other parts of Asia. Like Germany, Korea was a divided country with the northern zone under Soviet influence and the southern zone under the Americans, this situation eventually leading to the Korean War in 1950.

The American fear of communist subversion at home has been described as verging on hysteria. The excesses it stimulated can be seen most clearly in the work of the House Un-American Activities Committee (HUAC) and McCarthyism. The HUAC, a Congressional investigative committee established in 1938, is best remembered for the Hollywood Blacklist, a list of those involved in the entertainment business who were barred from working because of alleged communist or left-leaning political sympathies. The list was begun in 1947 and included scores of film directors, actors and writers. McCarthyism was named after Joseph McCarthy, a little known Republican Senator who came to attention in 1950 when he claimed to be able to name 205 Communist Party members working in the US Department of State. He became chairman of an investigative committee in 1953 and conducted a twelve-month campaign against the political left in America. Those he accused included government employees and academics. He was eventually discredited when he targeted a senior army officer but not before the fear of the 'red menace' had created a wave of hysteria throughout the country. 'Worrying about Communism was an exhaustingly demanding business in the 1950s', according to the humorist Bill Bryson who was a young boy in Iowa at the time. 'Red danger lurked everywhere.'[9] The playwright Arthur Miller, one of those accused of communist sympathies commented that the USA, with the tiniest Communist Party in the world, 'was behaving as though on the verge of bloody revolution'.[10]

The Berlin Blockade

Amongst all this turbulence, in 1948 the world was rocked by the Berlin Blockade, one of the early Cold War's most significant and dramatic events that set the global political atmosphere for some years to come. Three years after peace in Europe had been declared, Stalin retaliated against moves by the Western powers to create a divided Germany. The previous year, the British and Americans had united their German zones, with the French zone following soon after. A new currency was introduced into the united zones, contrary to the Potsdam agreement. Currencies are the visible economic symbol of an independent nation, a point that was not missed by the Kremlin. To make matters worse from the Russian point of view, moves were being made to introduce this new Deutschmark into the western sectors of Berlin, a city that was legally not a part of any of the German zones. In an attempt to stop these moves towards a new German state in the west, Stalin took drastic measures. He imposed a blockade on Berlin, refusing to allow the Western powers access to the city by road, rail or waterways. The effect of this action was that the inhabitants of the western sectors of Berlin were cut off from the West and could no longer be supplied with food, fuel and essential goods by the Western powers.

In propaganda terms the blockade turned out to be an own goal for Stalin. The Americans in particular presented his actions as a barbarous attempt to force a change of policy by starving the two million or so inhabitants of the city. The Americans and the British organised an airlift of essential goods. Planes flew into West Berlin airports around the clock for eleven months, bringing everything needed to keep a major city alive. In May 1949, Stalin backed down and opened up the transport crossings again. The airlift was hailed as an enormous success, a humanitarian victory for the Western powers and the citizens of the western part of Berlin against communism and its brutalities.

But the Berlin Blockade was the first major myth of the Cold War. The plight of the city was exaggerated by the West for propaganda purposes. Doubts about the validity of the picture presented in the Western media have been raised as new archive material has shown that West Berlin was never truly isolated. The blockade took place many years before the Berlin Wall created a solid and visible division between East and West. The western sectors of Berlin were not cut off from the Soviet sector or the surrounding countryside which came within the Soviet occupied zone. The people of the western sectors were able to obtain supplies from their east zone cousins, a fact which was secretly acknowledged by the Americans at the time. A report to Washington by US intelligence services in Berlin in October 1948 noted that the vast majority of the needs of those in the western sectors was being met by east-west trade, and that this trade was as necessary to the Soviet sector as it was to the western parts.[11] The Soviet Union even offered food to West Berliners, the offer being dismissed as 'propaganda' in July 1948 by General Lucius Clay, the US officer in charge of the airlift. 'The air lift has increased our prestige immeasurably ... Two months ago the Russians were cocky and arrogant. Lately they have been polite and have gone out of their way to avoid incidents', he wrote.[12] West Berliners knew about the Soviet offer but most of them turned it down, either because of the criticism they faced for accepting, or simply because the supply points were too far from home.

The significance of the Berlin Blockade is that it solidified the division of Europe. It was a trial of strength between East and West and it was clear to the voting public of the Western democracies which side they would rather be on. By the time the crisis ended both West Germans and West Berliners were firmly in the Western camp. That which Stalin had feared had become a reality. During the first half of 1949, both the North Atlantic Treaty Organisation (NATO) and the Federal Republic of Germany (West Germany) were established, the one a defensive Western alliance, the other the final nail in the coffin of a united Germany. Later that year the Kremlin followed suit and the Soviet zone of Germany became the GDR. Two German states had been created from the devastation of the Second World War; the one a client state of the USA and Britain, the other of the Soviet Union. The Iron Curtain had become a reality.

The people protest

By the 1950s trouble was brewing on the eastern side of the Iron Curtain. The people of the Soviet bloc in Europe were voicing their discontent with the people's republics in which they lived. Revolts took place in the GDR, Poland and Hungary between 1953 and 1956, triggered, to a certain extent, by the death of Stalin in 1953 and his subsequent denunciation by the new man in the Kremlin. Nikita Khrushchev was prepared to countenance modest reforms. By easing the lid on the pressure cooker, he provoked an explosion.

The workers of East Berlin were the first to take to the streets, ostensibly to protest against the lowering of already inadequate wages and shortages of essential goods. The uprising in the city was crushed within a matter of days by East German military police backed by Russian tanks but spread to other parts of the country. Recently available archive material has shown that the revolt was far more extensive and serious than was thought in the West at the time.[13] It was also significant because its essential elements were to be repeated in the revolts that followed elsewhere. One of the main questions that has not yet been answered definitively is who was behind it. Was it a genuinely spontaneous outburst by the workers against communist domination? This is the way it was presented to Western audiences with *The Times* telling its readers: 'East Berlin Demonstrators Shout for Freedom'. Was it orchestrated by the CIA? Or was it a convoluted plot by the Russians to rid themselves of the troublesome Ulbricht following Stalin's death and abandon the GDR to the capitalist West?

This latter theory is the most startling to Western minds conditioned to see the Soviet Union as an aggressive expansionist power. It is based on the fact that Stalin's head of secret police, Lavrenti Beria, was involved in a power struggle for the Soviet leadership following Stalin's death. Beria, it was alleged by his rivals, was in favour of abandoning the GDR to the West and some suspected that Beria's agents instigated the riots in Berlin. Beria was executed in December 1953, accused of conspiring to restore capitalism in the Soviet Union and plotting to destroy the GDR.[14] Although this conspiracy theory is generally discounted, its significance was that Russian policy towards Germany changed from one of being prepared to consider a neutral unified demilitarised Germany to a firm commitment to retain and strengthen the GDR. In this sense, Ulbricht won the day.

There is evidence to support the theory of US involvement in the riots, as was claimed by the East German regime at the time. US intelligence services did indeed attempt to subvert Soviet bloc countries, although the aim was to create instability rather than bring about regime change. A revolution that could drag the USA and Britain into an armed conflict in Europe was the last thing wanted. The stated aim of US psychological warfare in the region was to nourish resistance without compromising its spontaneous nature.

One of the main instruments used to do this was the radio station known as RIAS (Radio In the American Sector), based in West Berlin, staffed by Germans but under US control. One American official described the station as 'the spiritual and psychological center of resistance in a Communist-dominated, blacked-out area'.[15] It was RIAS which kept East German citizens informed about the revolt which was taking place and encouraged others to support the demonstrators in East Berlin.

Unfortunately, US propaganda about liberating the East Germans from the communist yoke was believed not only by those in the West but also by East Germans themselves, many of whom expected a Cold War version of the American cavalry to appear on the horizon. It is reported that some East German farmers at the time were refusing to sell their cattle, saying they would get a better price for them when the Americans arrived.[16] Living up to its own propaganda was a problem for the USA. Having failed to give anything other than rhetorical support to the demonstrators, Washington looked for a way of salvaging its reputation and hit upon the idea of providing food parcels for the hard pressed population of the GDR. The parcels, known as 'Eisenhower packages' were handed out from distribution centres in West Berlin. The plan was a huge success. East Germans flocked in their thousands to pick up their parcels. Whole villages and factories took to the trains and any form of transport they could find to make the journey to the distribution centres. Even Party members joined in the bonanza. The Americans basked in their beneficence while the Russians and East German authorities fumed but did little to stop it happening. The operation eventually foundered on the disapproval of the British and French who had always been opposed to this blatant form of propaganda and who were more interested in international stability than winning over the hearts and minds of the East Germans. US diplomats also opposed the scheme. They advised that sitting down with the Russians to talk about German unity would be more damaging to Soviet morale than 'getting the entire Soviet Zone population into West Berlin for a turkey dinner'.[17]

The Berlin Uprising provided a blueprint for the upheavals which followed in Poland and Hungary in 1956. The difference between the 1956 revolts was that whereas Hungary erupted into full-scale and bloody revolution, the Polish protest was contained relatively easily and without Soviet intervention.

Disturbances in Poznan near the Polish–GDR border were sparked off in June, again by dissatisfaction with wages and living standards, but were short lived. Although the demonstrations were suppressed with considerable violence by the Polish authorities, Soviet forces were not used. Discontent simmered but did not intensify or spread. The Polish Prime Minister, Boleslaw Bierut, had died in March, his demise making way for a new leader. In keeping with the more liberal atmosphere wafting east from Moscow, in October Wladyslaw Gomulka was chosen as the country's new leader. For the Polish people, he was a man with some credibility. Although a committed communist, he was seen as a nationalist and a liberal and had been imprisoned for his views for four years until 1955. The people's trust in Gomulka together with the fact that he was able to introduce some limited and controlled reforms helped to account for the manner in which the Polish uprising fizzled out.[18]

This was not the case in Hungary where unrest in October led to Soviet tanks in the streets of Budapest, bloodshed, arrests and a mass exodus of Hungarian dissidents. The preceding three years had seen a power struggle in Hungary between the hardline communist, Matyas Rákosi, and his more liberal rival, Imre Nagy. Rákosi, back in power in 1955, was deposed on Moscow's orders following Khrushchev's denunciation of Stalin but this apparent attempt at appeasement only intensified the demands of the dissidents. The revolution began on 23 October when students took to the streets demanding free elections, the withdrawal of Soviet troops and the introduction of a multiparty system. This was not a revolt against socialism but a demand for a liberalisation of the system. The Hungarian authorities, unlike the Poles, were unable to control the unrest. As the situation worsened, the decision was made to send in Soviet troops. The tanks met with much stiffer resistance than had been the case in East Berlin. Their presence alone did not quell the rioting and the order was given to open fire. Hungarian national pride, which had always been a major element in the unrest, was inflamed. The Kremlin dithered about the right course of action – to withdraw, as requested by Nagy, or to fight – but eventually withdrew on the grounds that propping up Nagy was the wiser course. However, talk of creating a neutral Hungary was too much for the Kremlin. With concerns about Polish stability still rife, there were fears that the Soviet bloc might crumble. Khrushchev ordered the Red Army to invade Hungary. The shelling of Budapest by Russian tanks began on 4 November. Thousands were killed or wounded. Thousands more were imprisoned or executed and more than 200,000 refugees fled to the West. Nagy was replaced by János Kádár, a leading Hungarian communist whose political leanings fell between the liberalism of Nagy and the Stalinism of Rákosi. After a protracted trial, Nagy was executed in 1958.

As in Berlin, the Hungarians had been encouraged in their demands by US propaganda. Once again communist dissidents had been led to believe that they had American support. Once again an American backed radio station was their mouthpiece. This time it was Radio Free Europe (RFE). It is now thought that the Soviet crackdown on Hungary was probably precipitated by RFE, which announced Nagy's plan to withdraw from the Warsaw Pact ahead of his own announcement and gave the Russians the impression that Nagy, unlike Gomulka, was not in control.[19] Once again, communist dissidents were abandoned by a West which had few qualms about using them to undermine Soviet power but had no intention of risking a war in order to help them. In the case of Hungary, the situation was further complicated by the fact that on 31 October, while Hungarian students were fighting Russian tanks on the streets of Budapest, the British and French were bombing the Suez Canal. The world turned its back on Hungary at a crucial moment in its history. By doing so the West demonstrated that the concept of rollback in Europe was dead. The occupation of Hungary by Soviet troops without Western intervention was an acknowledgement that the world was divided into spheres of influence and that Eastern Europe fell within the Soviet sphere. Opposition forces within the region were forced to recognise that for the foreseeable future the status quo prevailed.

The Berlin Wall

The erection of the Berlin Wall in 1961 together with its demolition in 1989 were probably the most iconic events of the Cold War. This is the image which illustrates the Cold War most vividly; the Brandenburg Gate towering above the ugly concrete structure, armed guards ready to shoot would-be escapers. Overnight families were parted, loved ones separated. Human tragedies were legion as the reality of Cold War politics touched the lives of millions of ordinary people. In the West, the building of the Berlin Wall was portrayed as a humanitarian crime which took the world by surprise. For the Soviet Union and East Germany it was another propaganda own goal. Now you can see the reality of communism, Westerners were able to say. They have to imprison their people behind barbed wire and concrete and shoot them if they try to escape. Two days after the wall went up, *The Times* told its readers:

> The East German Government has now made an open confession of failure. By virtually closing the frontier between east and west Berlin, which was the main escape route for refugees, it has admitted that its country is such a thoroughly unpleasant and inefficient place in which to live that its unhappy citizens must be kept there by force. Its protestations that the west German Government was luring people across by some sort of trickery will carry little weight anywhere, least of all in east Germany itself. The plain fact is that some 2,500,000 people have left it since 1949.

The official East German line was that the construction was an 'anti-Fascist protection wall', built not to keep Easterners in but to keep Westerners out. West Berlin provided Western intelligence agencies with an invaluable hole through the Iron Curtain. However, Ulbricht's most pressing concern was to stop the flood of refugees west, draining his country of resources.[20] It was professional, skilled and well-educated East Germans to whom the West held out its hand. A GDR joke at the time had one East German saying to another: 'Do you know that legally you can now go to West Germany twice a year – once to see your doctor and once to see your dentist'. This attitude was so pervasive that the joke was recorded by the Stasi in its file on the Secretary of State for Church Affairs, noting that his wife had told it to a friend and was therefore politically unreliable.[21]

The West's reaction to the building of the wall was totally underwhelming. It was indeed a huge propaganda coup for the West and, as the years went by, the West's hand-wringing over this crime against the people and the myth of its opposition to the wall grew ever stronger. But the reality was that at the time the West heaved a huge sigh of relief. Now, at last, perhaps things would stabilise. Now, perhaps the problem of Berlin could be put on the back burner. Willy Brandt, at that time Mayor of West Berlin and later to become West German Chancellor, expressed his astonishment at the West's lack of reaction. 'Ulbricht had been allowed to take a swipe at the Western super-power,' he wrote, 'and the United State merely winced with annoyance'.[22] President Kennedy did not interrupt his yachting holiday. Prime Minister Macmillan left for his shooting holiday in Yorkshire two days after the wall went up. Crisis? What crisis?

There was a belated confrontation between US and Soviet tanks across the border crossing of Checkpoint Charlie two months later, a confrontation probably contrived by the Americans and which then escalated. Kennedy had no desire to turn the Berlin Wall into an international incident but, as a symbol of US resolve, he sent General Clay, the man behind the Berlin airlift, back to the city. Clay favoured a stronger line. The Russians began to fear that the Americans might attempt to bulldoze their way through the wall. The standoff began when an American diplomat and his wife tried to cross the border to attend the opera in the east and were turned back when they refused to show their passports. Kennedy reportedly commented with some annoyance that the diplomat had not been sent to Berlin in order to go to the opera. But the incident turned into a dangerous trial of strength with tanks from both sides massing at the border. The Americans claimed victory when, after a few days, the Soviet tanks withdrew. However, it is now known that Kennedy was the first to hold out an olive branch, sending a secret message to Khrushchev saying that the Americans would withdraw if the Russians did likewise.[23]

The truth was that both the British and the Americans were relieved that all that had happened was that Ulbricht had built a wall. It could have been much worse. Since 1958 Khrushchev had increasingly been using Berlin as a lever with which to bully the West. The period between 1958 and 1961 has become known as the Berlin Crisis. Khrushchev handed out ultimatums, the allies stalled, tensions rose, no one knew where it would all end. As Brandt remarked: 'What we in Berlin regarded as a cruel blow may almost have come as a relief to others.' There is reason to suspect that the Western allies had been warned in advance that Ulbricht was going to divide the city. These doubts were raised at the time and have become more frequent. Brandt asserts that what happened on 13 August was 'not a bolt from the blue'. The possibility of such action was in the air. The influential Labour politician, Richard Crossman, who acted as a secret link between Britain and the GDR, was in East Berlin the day before the building of the wall began and asked a senior member of the GDR government why Ulbricht was not doing more to close off the East–West border. More 'energetic steps' were needed, he said.[24] A few days earlier he had told a leading Party member that he could not understand why the GDR did not shut the border in order to put a stop to the West Germans enticing East German workers away.

The 1950s had been a period of adjustment in Europe. With the ending of the Second World War, the former allies had been confronted with a totally new situation in which the two major political systems which had survived the war, communism and capitalism, met head to head. Fear and suspicion had coloured international relations. The rhetoric from both sides had been aggressive. But as the dust settled on a divided Europe, a new tone of realism could be heard. The talk was not of rollback or containment but of the preservation of the status quo. The uprisings in East Berlin, Poland and Hungary had demonstrated the emptiness of Western rhetoric, particularly that of America, about freeing the people of Eastern Europe. These revolts had all been nourished by the USA, which had then refused to go to the aid of the Germans, Poles and Hungarians who had naively believed the propaganda. Instead, the USA had stood piously on the sidelines, crying crocodile tears over troubles it had helped to foment and accusing the Russians of brutally crushing spontaneous cries for freedom.

After these disasters, the Berlin Wall was a relief. It sealed the division of Europe and paved the way for a more stable continent. It offered up the chance of a permanent reduction in tension. What the world wanted by the 1960s was stability. A new word was gaining currency: it was détente. The myths, nevertheless, persisted. It was a myth that the Soviet Union was responsible for the division of Europe; it was a myth that the Marshall Plan was purely a charitable act by the USA to save Western Europe; it was a myth that West Berlin was isolated during the Berlin Blockade; it was a myth that the uprisings in the GDR, Poland and Hungary during the 1950s were spontaneous; and above all it was a myth that the West was shocked by the building of the Berlin Wall. It would be some time before the ordinary man in the street would become aware of the political change of tone. For him the myths were his reality.

4

The thaw: détente in Europe

The first decade and a half of the Cold War in Europe was a time of turbulence. The Soviet Union and the USA resembled two adolescents squaring up to each other on the school playground, both nervous about throwing the first punch but both wanting to look tough in front of their watching class-mates. There was plenty of name calling and a few exploratory blows were exchanged as the two searched for a weakness to exploit. But they were fairly evenly matched and both came to realise that they risked their own destruction if it came to a fight at close quarters. By the beginning of the 1960s little had been gained by this sparring other than a clearer definition of territor-ial boundaries. The awareness was dawning that brain rather than brawn might be the way to achieve victory.

Thus it was that the next fifteen years of the Cold War in Europe took on the appearance of relative tranquillity. After the blustering of the 1950s, the protagonists began to examine ways in which they could co-exist. This did not mean that there was any lessening of ideological hostility; rather, it meant that both sides focused their attentions on more subtle ways of subverting the enemy. Instead of raising international tension, East and West looked at ways of reducing it through a policy known as détente.

The age of détente is frequently dated from the late 1960s and into the 1970s. This was indeed a time of overt activity when high-level summits and international treaties made it evident to all that an accommodation was taking place between East and West. But, increasingly, evidence suggests that détente was in the air many years earlier. On the capitalist side, this was particularly the case in Europe with the British secretly talking about détente for traditional pragmatic reasons, the West Germans forging their own links with their eastern brethren, and the French taking an independent anti-American line which opened the door to Moscow. The Russians too were prepared to use the word 'détente' in private many years before it could be spoken of publicly. It was the USA which dragged its heels, adopting a bellicose attitude while European diplomats were quietly working away behind the scenes to establish a way of living together. It was, of course, difficult for political leaders on both sides of the Iron Curtain to reconcile the policy of détente with the aggressive rhetoric that had been fed to the general public in the 1950s. In the West, it took time to explain to the electorate that the evil enemy of yesterday had become the trading partner of today. In the East, it was not the electorate which needed to be seduced but the political hardliners within the Soviet hierarchy.

Ironically, it was the event which brought the world to the brink of nuclear war, the Cuban missile crisis, which strengthened the hand of the advocates of détente. Hardliners on both sides of the Iron Curtain lost ground as politicians and people saw how close they had come to mutual destruction. The Cuban missile crisis, which will be examined in detail in chapter 6, was the seminal event of détente. It was a frightening demonstration of what could happen if the world continued on its confrontational course.

But détente was not a synonym for peace. Cold War conflicts continued around the world, not least in Vietnam. In Europe too there were explosive moments, the invasion of Czechoslovakia by Soviet and Warsaw Pact troops in 1968 demonstrating not only Russia's determination to retain a grip on her sphere of influence but also, once again, the West's reluctance to interfere on the side of European dissidents. In addition, détente did not mean a lessening of the ideological struggle between capitalism and communism. On the contrary, the purity of capitalist or communist ideology became increasingly important as the two sides grew closer together in the practical areas of trade and arms reduction.

Learning to live together

Pragmatism is an attribute for which British foreign policy makers have long been renowned. The Cold War was no exception. At a time when the Americans were digging themselves ever deeper into the trench of ideological paranoia and hostility, the British were secretly talking about cosying up to the Russians. There were occasions during the 1950s when the British Foreign Office feared that American recklessness was more likely to provoke a global war than Russian aggression.[1] The rationale behind the British approach was that seduction rather than confrontation was the better way to defeat communism. This philosophy can be seen in a major top secret Cabinet analysis of the future of the world over the next decade, drawn up in 1960, which advised that: 'The best, perhaps the only, hope for a peaceful end to the East–West conflict, is that the East should mellow into a bourgeois prosperity where it will lose its urge to win the world for Communism ... we must do anything we can to assist the process.'[2] In other words, turn communists into consumers and the problem will resolve itself. The report continued:

> China has not yet evolved to a point where anything can be done, but Russia presents greater opportunities: visits, meetings, cultural or commercial exchanges are small steps in that direction ... [Communist ideology] can best be eroded away by

exposure to another system which is shown to be equally successful and more attractive.

In addition, it was recommended that Britain should not oppose all things Russian as a matter of principle. 'We need not necessarily disagree with the Russians at every point. There will be a common interest in controlling situations which could lead to global war and, perhaps, working for a measure of disarmament.'

For the Russians too, the idea of détente being preferable to confrontation can be detected in their covert machinations during the early years of the Cold War, as the overt conflict hotted up. They even used one of the West's greatest espionage debacles in order to put across the message of détente. In a joint spying exercise known as Operation Gold, British and American intelligence agencies had dug a secret tunnel underneath Berlin during the mid-1950s. The tunnel ran from the American Sector to the Soviet Sector and provided the West with a means of tapping into Soviet communications systems. For more than a year, Western spies diligently eavesdropped on the Russians until in 1956 the Soviet end of the tunnel was stormed by Russian and East German soldiers. What the West did not know, was that the Russians had known about the tunnel all along. One of those involved in its planning was the British double agent George Blake who was convicted of spying for the Soviet Union in 1961. He had alerted the Russians to the tunnel in its planning stages but they had allowed it to continue so that they could feed information, as they saw fit, to the West. Probably the most important aspect of this operation was that the Russians, knowing that the British and Americans were listening, deliberately put over a message designed to reassure 'the West that the Soviet's intentions were not bellicose'.[3] Sceptics would argue that this was pure disinformation intended merely to encourage the West to lower its guard. But given the difficult economic and political circumstances that the Soviet Union was experiencing in the post-Second World War years, Stalin's desire for peace is plausible.

The secret agenda of subversion behind détente, as spelled out by British foreign policy makers, was echoed by their Soviet counterparts. According to the newspaper *Izvestia*, the mouthpiece of the Soviet government, détente was 'a form of peaceful coexistence in which the political and economic struggle is damped down in favour of a relaxation in tensions and economic co-operation, but in which ideological struggle survives and acquires new importance'.[4] Just as the furtherance of capitalism was a central tenet of the Western form of détente, so was communism and its eventual spread essential to the Russian view of détente or, as they often referred to it, peaceful co-existence.

> Peaceful co-existence does not at all mean an end to the rivalry between the two world social systems. The struggle between the proletariat and the bourgeoisie, between world socialism and imperialism, will go on until the final and complete victory of communism on a worldwide scale. The Soviet Communist Party (CPSU) has proceeded and proceeds now from the fact that class struggle between two systems – capitalist and socialist – in the economic and political spheres and, naturally, in the sphere of ideology will continue.[5]

Thus spoke *Pravda*, the official organ of the Soviet Communist Party. Soviet interpretation of détente was a mirror image of that of the West. Like their Western counterparts, Soviet leaders saw increased trade with capitalist countries and cultural exchanges as an opportunity to infiltrate and subvert. The Soviet leader, Leonid Brezhnev, told a Russian audience that he was convinced that 'the expansion of cultural values and information, the development of ties between the peoples of various countries – all this being natural in conditions of détente – will greatly help to spread the truth about socialism and to win more and more adherents over to the side of the ideas of scientific communism'.[6]

The American attitude to détente in the 1960s was fairly muted. As the decade progressed the escalation of the conflict in Vietnam made it difficult to hear the voices of those who preached tolerance and co-existence. Détente policy was further weakened by the sudden death of the man who was trying to change the course of US policy. Kennedy's keynote speech marking a potential shift in Cold War attitudes was made to American University, Washington DC in June 1963, one year after the Cuban missile crisis. His subject was world peace. Although the word 'détente' was not mentioned, he called for tolerance, better understanding between the Soviet Union and the USA and increased contact and communication. 'Total war makes no sense in an age where great powers can maintain large and relatively invulnerable nuclear forces,' he told his audience. 'Some say that it is useless to speak of world peace ... until the leaders of the Soviet Union adopt a more enlightened attitude. I hope they do. I believe we can help them do it. But I also believe that we must reexamine our own attitude ... for our attitude is as essential as theirs.'[7] Continuing this major change of rhetoric, he went on to tell his audience that:

> no government or social system is so evil that its people must be considered as lacking in virtue ... We are both caught up in a vicious and dangerous cycle in which suspicion on one side breeds suspicion on the other, and new weapons beget counter-weapons ... We must, therefore, persevere in the search for peace in the hope that constructive changes within the Communist bloc might bring within reach solutions which now seem beyond us.

The speech was well received in both London and Moscow. It was described as eloquent and welcome and Kennedy was praised for also addressing 'a few words of sanity' to his own people. 'Neither of the protagonists in the cold war finds it easy to assess the true aims of the other. Both are to some extent prisoners of their own propaganda', *The Times* opined. Khrushchev described the speech as 'a step forward in a realistic appraisal of the international situation' and called for practical deeds to back up these 'good statements', particularly in the areas of economic ties and the development of trade.[8] A hotline between Washington and Moscow was opened on 30 August 1963. Five months later Kennedy was dead, murdered by an assassin in Dallas, Texas on 22 November 1963. Khrushchev was ousted by his rivals in Moscow eleven months later.

The creeping move towards co-operation in Europe during the 1960s was also on the German agenda. Indeed, the attitude of the two German states, West Germany and the GDR, was a major factor in the emergence of European détente. The policy that was developed became known as Ostpolitik. The man whose name is most closely associated with Ostpolitik was Willy Brandt, leader of the West German socialist party (SPD), mayor of West Berlin from 1957 to 1966 and West German Chancellor from 1969 to 1974. In his position as West Berlin mayor, Brandt was involved in putting out feelers to Khrushchev shortly after the Berlin Wall was built. This had to be done with the utmost caution, given West Germany's rigid refusal to recognise the existence of the GDR and its policy (known as the Hallstein Doctrine) of isolating any other country which did. The merest hint that a West German politician might entertain the idea of talking to the Russians, let alone the East Germans, was enough to arouse the ire of the ruling establishment. In 1963, a secret meeting between Brandt and Khrushchev was planned in East Berlin. But Brandt was forced to cancel the meeting at the eleventh hour when word of it leaked out to his political rivals. 'My sole course was to decline at the last minute', Brandt wrote later. 'I found it hard. Khrushchev must have taken my refusal as an affront.'[9]

In his place, Brandt sent two German Church leaders. The use of intermediaries in this manner was not uncommon in the conditions of the Cold War, which often meant that political leaders could not be seen to be talking to each other. Church leaders were popular messengers. Their calling and membership of the international Christian network meant that they could cross borders, even the Iron Curtain, without too many questions being asked. On this occasion, the message the Church leaders gave to Khrushchev was that despite the icy relations that existed between the two Germanys and between West Germany and the Soviet Union, there were West Germans who were prepared to talk to the Russians, albeit in secret.[10]

Later that year, Brandt's close colleague, Egon Bahr, who is credited with the intellectual formulation of Ostpolitik, went public with this policy, describing it as *Wandel durch Annäherung* (change through rapprochement), a phrase which became common parlance in Europe. Like the British and the Russians, Brandt and his colleagues saw co-operation as a way of achieving their goal not only of defeating communism but also of bringing about the eventual reunification of Germany. They had taken note of events in Hungary, Poland and East Berlin in the 1950s and realised that communist regimes could not be overthrown by internal revolt. They concluded there had to be another way.

The advocates of Ostpolitik were much criticised by fellow West Germans for negotiating with the communists. In 1970, when Brandt finally recognised the state borders of the GDR, he and his colleagues were accused of betraying the East German people, of abandoning them to their fate. But they argued that it was necessary to accept the geopolitical status quo before change could be brought about. As with détente, though, ideological struggle was central to Ostpolitik. The aim in Bahr's words, was to bring about the 'dissolution of the ideological cement' that held communist states together.[11] The goal was long-term, Bahr and his colleagues anticipating that it would be ten to twenty years at least before such a policy would have visible effect. But events that took place in Prague in 1968 raise the question of whether the ideological subversion of Ostpolitik had an effect sooner than anticipated. Were the Czechs unwittingly ahead of the agenda?

Prague Spring

It was in August 1968 that Soviet tanks once again rolled into a European country in order to crush an uprising. This time it was Czechoslovakia which was to learn that, despite reductions in international tension and talk of socialism with a human face, when it came to the crunch Moscow still retained its grip. The immediate crisis began when Alexander Dubček took control of the Czech Communist Party in January 1968 and announced his intention of introducing liberalising reforms such as a relaxation of censorship. Three months later, the Communist Party published an action plan calling for democratisation of the political and economic system. It envisaged, for example, that Czechoslovakia would no longer be a one party state. The reforms were greeted with enthusiasm by Czechs but viewed with alarm by the leaders of Czechoslovakia's communist neighbours. Was this liberalisation disease infectious, they wondered? Ulbricht, in the GDR, and Gomulka, in Poland, urged Brezhnev to take action. Czech leaders were called to Moscow in May to be told of Soviet concerns and in June, in what was seen as an attempt to reinforce the point, Warsaw Pact military exercises were held in Czechoslovakia.

In August, Soviet bloc leaders met in Bratislava and agreed that it was the right and the duty of other communist countries to intervene in another communist country if Marxist–Leninist ideology was threatened by bourgeois capitalist forces. This statement of intent became known as the Brezhnev Doctrine. Although Czechoslovakia's strategically important position, on the frontline of the Iron Curtain and sharing a border with West Germany and Austria, was considered to be a part of the equation when the decision was finally made to invade, it appears that the deciding factor was ideological rather than military. Justifying the invasion, Brezhnev told Polish workers later that year that: 'The weakening of any of the links in the world system of socialism directly affects all the socialist countries, which cannot look indifferently upon this.'[12] This maxim became one of the basic tenets of Soviet foreign policy until Gorbachev rejected it in 1989 – with dramatic results.

Troops from five Warsaw Pact countries (Romania was opposed to intervention and did not take part) entered Czechoslovakia on 20 August 1968. The Russians claimed that leading Czech politicians had 'invited' the troops in, fearing a 'counter-revolution'. Dubček and others were arrested and taken to Moscow while crowds confronted the tanks in Prague's Wenceslas Square. Dubček was persuaded to renounce the reforms and agree to the presence of Soviet troops in Czechoslovakia. Western countries issued protests but did nothing. Dubček was allowed to return to Prague as leader with instructions to reverse his own reforms. On 16 January 1969, a student, Jan Palach, died when he set himself on fire in protest in Wenceslas Square. A second student, Jan Zajíc, died in the same way a month later. Dubček himself was replaced in April 1969 by a hardliner, Gustáv Husák, backed by the Soviet Union. A period of what was called 'normalisation' followed during which the reform movement was suppressed.

Why did it happen, this Prague Spring, this brief period of euphoria, the scent of which wafted through Czechoslovakia in April 1968? What led to the creation of the reform movement and why did the Czechs seem to believe that they would be allowed to transform the political, economic and social systems of their country? Had they learned nothing from events in Hungary and East Berlin? Was it Russian inaction in the first half of 1968 that led the Czechs to believe that their liberalisation movement would be tolerated? Why did the Russians dither again? Why did they leave Dubček in power and then return him to power after the invasion? And why did the West effectively turn a blind eye to the invasion of Czechoslovakia?

These are some of the puzzling aspects to events in Prague in 1968 and the answers to the questions they raise are many and varied. Essentially, though, they can be distilled into one word – détente. The main priority of both the Soviet Union and the West at that time was the furtherance of détente, the preservation of stability and the status quo. A British Foreign Office Minister summed it up when he commented that British interests would not be served by 'major disturbances' similar to those in Hungary and Poland in 1956. 'A general anti-communist upheaval would', he argued, 'undermine the "evolution of effective co-existence" which would provide the basis upon which East–West détente would rest.'[13] US President Lyndon Johnson has been quoted as describing the Czech affair as 'an accident on the road to détente'.[14]

In any case, neither superpower was focusing on Czechoslovakia at the time. The USA was in trouble in Vietnam; the Russians were worried about developments in China and, closer to home, the maverick behaviour of Nicolae Ceauşescu in Romania. In addition, France, West Germany and the USA were distracted by their own domestic revolutions that were taking place on the streets of Paris, Chicago and Bonn as the young post-war generation made its voice heard.

Ironically, détente not only explains the reaction to the Prague Spring but also helps to explain why it happened in the first place. The political philosophy which encouraged a reduction in international tension also encouraged the Czechs to

the generally more relaxed mood of the time
.em as well. Détente, as was intended, had encour-
.e contact between East and West; it had enabled the
lib. .deas of the capitalist world to penetrate the Iron Curtain,
just as British foreign policy makers had anticipated eight years
before. The Czechs who led the Prague Spring were not anti-
communists. Indeed they included the Czech communist leader
Dubček. This was not revolt from below but from above. It was
not a move to rid the country of Marxist dogma but to change
it, to breathe new life into it, to create, as Dubček famously
described it, socialism with a human face. This was evolution,
not revolution, but the major players on the world stage
were slow to see the threat that Czech evolution presented to
stability.

One of the most influential underground East–West
networks operating in Czechoslovakia revolved around the
Protestant and Catholic Churches. Communist intelligence
services were deeply interested in the new ideology of
Christian–Marxist dialogue which had gained ground throughout Europe during the 1960s. It saw this doctrine as seriously
subversive. Prague was a centre of the Christian–Marxist
dialogue movement, the home of the international talking shop
known as the Christian Peace Conference which was attended
by Marxists and Christians from both sides of the Iron Curtain.
This organisation was a part of the intellectual movement
behind the Prague Spring. A Stasi report noted, for example,
that the contacts being made in Czechoslovakia were similar to
those that had preceded events in Hungary in 1956.[15] It listed the
names of Czech academics who were active in the underground
network and in close and constant contact with German Church
organisations, regarded by the Stasi as subversive.[16] One of its
reports, for example, quoted a West German Church leader,
suspected of being behind subversive networks and, indeed,
working for Western intelligence agencies, in an unguarded

moment telling one of its secret informers that: 'There really is a liberal wing in communism today, although it sounds like a paradox. It is amazing the way that liberalism has broken out in the CSSR [Czechoslovakia], which used to be the most pig-headed country in the Eastern bloc ... there is a younger generation there who say "What are the dopes up there wanting, who don't seem to realise that things must change".'[17]

During the 1960s, there was a mushrooming of ideological exchanges in various disciplines – economic, philosophical, political, religious. These exchanges were a part of the way in which the ideological cement of communism, referred to by Egon Bahr, was chipped away. The exchanges were taking place in other countries too. Poland, the GDR and even the Soviet Union were targeted by Western institutions interested in bringing about a change in the world order. But one of the most important factors from a Western perspective was that the cement should be removed in a planned and controlled manner. If it was removed too quickly there was a danger that the equilibrium of the world order would be disturbed in a manner which would lead to chaos and anarchy. The Czechs, it seems, were ahead of the agenda. Its leaders and its people had embraced the message of reform too enthusiastically. The cement was crumbling, bringing the buildings down before new structures were ready to replace them. It was a situation that troubled both East and West. There was, therefore, a tacit understanding that the Czechoslovakians should be forced to revert to the status quo.

Détente as official policy

The second stage of détente began after the Prague Spring with the election of Richard Nixon as US President in 1968 and Willy Brandt as West German Chancellor in 1969. Both men

were committed to their own versions of détente, the one focus-
ing on China and agreements on arms control, the other on the
GDR. During the late 1960s and early 1970s, significant agreements were reached between East and West. In November
1969, the USA and the Soviet Union began talks aimed at
restraining the arms race. The Strategic Arms Limitation Talks
(SALT) continued until May 1972 and resulted in the signing of
SALT 1, which limited defensive anti-ballistic missile systems.
By 1970, Moscow had signed a non-aggression pact with West
Germany, the result of secret negotiations with Brandt's right-
hand man, Bahr. The Moscow Treaty marked the start of the
official version of Ostpolitik. The West Germans, despite much
domestic opposition, agreed to recognise the border between

Talks between the Soviet Union and the USA aimed at restraining
the arms race began in November 1969. These talks culminated in
May 1972 in what is commonly known as SALT 1 – the Strategic
Arms Limitation Treaty. A specific agreement under which a limit
was placed on the development of anti-ballistic missile systems was
known as the ABM Treaty (Anti-Ballistic Missile Treaty). The development of these weapons had threatened to have a destabilising
effect on nuclear deterrence. Further talks began in November
1974 seeking agreement on the number and types of missiles
possessed. These detailed negotiations culminated in SALT 2 in
June 1979. The two sides agreed to limitations on a variety of
strategic offensive weapons, including delivery systems. The treaty
was not ratified by the US Senate, partly in response to Russia's
invasion of Afghanistan at the end 1979, but nevertheless both
sides tended to abide by its limits. The Reagan administration
abandoned the SALT talks. In May 1982, new negotiations on arms
limitation began, known as Strategic Arms Reduction Talks or
START. Agreement was reached between Gorbachev and Reagan
in May 1988 following the signing of the Intermediate Range
Nuclear Forces Treaty the previous year.

the two German states as well as the GDR–Polish border, thus opening the way for better relations between the two German states.

Trade was another important piece of the Ostpolitik–détente jigsaw. Its significance can be seen most clearly in the trading relations between the two Germanys, but for other Soviet bloc countries too better trading relations with the West were not only desirable but necessary. The West saw trade as another way of influencing the communist bloc. As early as 1962, the US Secretary of State Dean Rusk had spoken of the need for West Germany to make East Germany economically dependent on it.[18] Bahr is reported to have said that trading relations not only contributed to peaceful relations with the East but were also a lever with which to transform it.[19] West Germany was prepared to offer the GDR advantageous trading terms, including guaranteed credit arrangements which helped the struggling GDR economy to survive but also put the country effectively in hock to the West. The GDR's requirement for hard currency also brought about a bizarre trade in people with East German dissidents being effectively 'sold' to the West. Ultimately, the East German Communist Party became dependent on West German credit arrangements.

One of the most important figures in the later stages of détente was Nixon's emissary and later Secretary of State, Henry Kissinger. He was responsible for paving the way towards an improvement in relations between the USA and China. In doing so he also brought the expression 'back channel' into the public lexicon – a diplomatic term for a secret channel of communication between states. Kissinger became the arch practitioner of back-channel diplomacy, the tool of realpolitik. He made his first secret visits to China in 1971, enabling Nixon to make his own official visit in 1972. Reflecting on back-channel diplomacy, Bahr, Kissinger's rival for the back-channel crown, described it as the necessary tool for governments which

The man who shaped American foreign policy during the middle years of the Cold War and whose style of diplomacy continues to influence the manner in which international affairs are conducted was a refugee from Nazi Germany. Born Heinz Alfred Kissinger in Bavaria in 1923, a child of the Weimar Republic and the son of Jewish parents, he was ten years old when Adolf Hitler became German Chancellor. In 1938 the family fled to America and Kissinger became a naturalised US citizen in 1943. He was drafted into the US army and served in the Counter Intelligence Corps in occupied Germany. Under a scheme to provide university education for returning veterans, Kissinger enrolled as a student at Harvard and subsequently became a Professor of Government there. In 1957 he published a study of the peacemakers of 1814–15 called *A World Restored: Castlereagh, Metternich and the Restoration of Peace* in which he laid out the general principles of the balance-of-power diplomacy for which he was to become renowned, first as Assistant to the President for National Security Affairs under Nixon from 1969 to 1975 and subsequently as Secretary of State from 1973 to 1977. In 1973, he was awarded the Nobel Peace Prize for his efforts to secure peace in Vietnam. He is known for his willingness to talk to the other side, the creator of what became known as 'the Channel', which enabled the Soviet Union and the USA to conduct secret negotiations. Kissinger's counterpart for many years was Anatoly Dobrynin, Soviet ambassador to the USA for twenty-four years until 1986. Dedicating his memoirs to Kissinger in 1995, he wrote: 'To Henry, opponent, partner, friend'. Kissinger is currently chairman of Kissinger Associates, an international consulting firm, and continues to write on global politics. In 2007, he wrote that the collapse of the American effort in Iraq would be a geopolitical calamity. He has also cautioned against the re-emergence of Cold War attitudes.

wish to 'create something new and want to create confidence'. It was through the use of back channels that the policies of détente and Ostpolitik were able to grow from the seeds planted at the beginning of the 1960s into the international co–operation which eventually led to something very new – the Helsinki agreements of 1975.

An enormous change took place in the global political atmosphere during the 1960s. At the start of the decade, the world had been hit by two major crises; the building of the Berlin Wall and the Cuban missile crisis. The division and hostility between the world's great power blocs had rarely seemed greater. Yet, by 1972 the President of the USA was shaking the hand of Zhou Enlai, one of the leaders of the communist world, and signing an arms limitation treaty with Brezhnev, the leader of the other great communist power. This transformation had come about thanks to the policy of détente and to the enormous efforts of those who had worked behind the scenes over many years in order to build trust and create channels of communication between countries which in public denounced each other. By the 1970s the world seemed to be moving into a new phase. On the surface at least it looked as though it was learning to live in peace. In 1973, world leaders from both sides of the Iron Curtain began talks in Helsinki aimed at reducing international tensions, these talks culminating in the Helsinki Accords in 1975. But the differences had not been resolved, they were merely better disguised. The inherent contradictions between the two systems remained. The world only appeared tranquil. In reality the Soviet bloc was being quietly undermined. In a world of smokescreens and mirrors, the hand of friendship could turn out to be bearing a poisoned chalice. So it was to prove with the next major development in international relations – the use of human rights as a political weapon.

5

Confrontation: the end of the Cold War in Europe

The curtain went up on the final act of the Cold War in the Finnish capital of Helsinki in 1975. It was there that thirty-five heads of state and political leaders from both sides of the Iron Curtain met to put their names to declarations of principle and intent concerning matters such as territorial integrity, security, economic and technological collaboration, and, most importantly, human rights. The Helsinki Accords on Security and Co-operation in Europe were a turning point. Fifteen years later the Cold War in Europe drew to a close. At the start of the 1980s, Poland had taken the lead in bringing about change, both through the activities of the independent trade union movement, Solidarity, and through the influence of the Polish cardinal who became the head of the Roman Catholic Church. By 1985, the wind of change was blowing through the Kremlin. The new man in power, Mikhail Gorbachev, spoke of glasnost (openness) and perestroika (reconstruction) and introduced reforms within the Soviet Union. The old guard in Eastern Europe had begun to lose its grip as the citizens of the communist bloc clamoured for freedom, and by the end of 1989 it was all but over. The Berlin Wall, the greatest symbol of divided Europe, had disintegrated into a pile of rubble.

Human rights and the Helsinki Accords

The concept of human rights dominated the final years of the Cold War in Europe in a way that it had failed to do during the periods of freeze and thaw. Despite the fact that, following the atrocities of the Second World War, human rights had been enshrined in the 30 Articles of the 1948 United Nations Universal Declaration of Human Rights, reaffirmed by the European Convention on Human Rights in 1950, these rights had played only a minor role in international relations and had had little immediate impact upon the average European citizen. Indeed there were worries in the West that commitments to human rights could create difficulties for countries such as Britain in their colonies. In a Cabinet discussion about the UN human rights declaration, for example, British Foreign Secretary Herbert Morrison commented that the human rights agenda had all started as anti-Soviet propaganda but could end up putting Britain 'on the spot' especially in the colonies.[1]

Following Helsinki, the protection of human rights became a legitimate part of diplomatic relations, an essential element of détente, and a fundamental plank of US foreign policy. At the time, many commentators considered the significance of Helsinki to be in its clauses relating to security and economics. It was only gradually that people in the West came to understand the leverage they had been handed by the Soviet Union's signature on documents guaranteeing human rights. Similarly, despite the fact that Moscow had sensed danger and had been reluctant to give its agreement to this aspect of the Helsinki Accords, only gradually did the Russians come to understand the power of the weapon that became a part of the capitalist arsenal.

Initially Western voices were raised against Helsinki. These agreements were a Soviet gain and a Western loss, critics said. President Gerald Ford and Kissinger were accused of endorsing

Soviet domination of Eastern Europe by recognising borders and spheres of influence in return for a mere non-binding nod in the direction of personal freedoms by Moscow. The dissident Russian writer Alexander Solzhenitsyn charged Ford with betraying Eastern Europe simply by attending the summit. Within the Soviet Union, the voices of those urging caution in relation to the human rights issue were drowned out by those who claimed that the West's recognition of Soviet hegemony far outweighed vague talk of human rights. Western supporters of Helsinki argued that the Kremlin was indeed being asked to give more than it received. The agreements would encourage people in the Soviet bloc to demand the rights and freedoms that had been laid out, they said; this proved to be the case.

The significance of human rights in the Cold War took on yet greater importance with the election of Jimmy Carter as US President in 1977. American foreign policy was at a low ebb following Vietnam and revelations about US support for right-wing dictators and assassination plots in Latin America. Partly in an attempt to win back the moral high ground, Carter made human rights the central plank of his foreign policy. Critics at the time and subsequently have accused him and his policy of being naive and simplistic. But his defenders have pointed out that the policy once again gave the USA, the home of the Bill of Rights, moral credibility around the world while at the same time putting Moscow on the defensive. Carter told the American people:

> Being confident of our own future, we are now free of that inordinate fear of communism which once led us to embrace any dictator who joined us in that fear ... For too many years, we've been willing to adopt the flawed and erroneous princi-ples and tactics of our adversaries, sometimes abandoning our own values for theirs. We've fought fire with fire, never think-ing that fire is better quenched with water. This approach

failed, with Vietnam the best example of its intellectual and moral poverty. But through failure we have now found our way back to our own principles and values, and we have regained our lost confidence ... we have reaffirmed America's commitment to human rights as a fundamental tenet of our foreign policy.[2]

The promotion of human rights by the West was crucial in turning the tide. By persuading the Kremlin to sign up to the Helsinki Accords, the West obtained a psychological weapon with which to exert pressure on Moscow and a means with which to undermine the Soviet bloc. As Carter's National Security Adviser, Zbigniew Brzezinski, was to remark post-Cold War: 'I readily concede that there was an element of tactical expediency in our own focus on human rights. The issue provided a powerful ideological weapon in the struggle against the Soviet Union and its communist doctrine.'[3]

Helsinki became a rallying point for Soviet bloc dissidents and, for the first time, raised the spectre of a unified opposition which crossed national borders and different interest groups.[4] Organisations were created to monitor and promote the rights that had been guaranteed, Human Rights Watch, which began life as Helsinki Watch in 1978, and Charter 77 in Czechoslovakia being two of the most prominent. Individuals who were critical of the Soviet system took strength from the fact that their voices were being heard and listened to in the West. After Helsinki, dissidents had an international profile. The Russian physicist and human rights activist Andrei Sakharov was awarded the Nobel Peace Prize only months after the Helsinki agreements were signed. The Soviet authorities refused to allow him to collect it in person but in an acceptance speech that was read for him by his wife he told a worldwide audience:

What made me particularly happy was to see that the commit-tee's decision stressed the link between defense of peace and defense of human rights, emphasizing that the defense of human rights guarantees a solid ground for genuine long-term international cooperation. Not only did you thus explain the meaning of my activity, but you also granted it a powerful support ... Granting the award to a person who defends political and civil rights against illegal and arbitrary actions means an affirmation of principles which play such an important role in determining the future of mankind. For hundreds of people, known or unknown to me, many of whom pay a high price for the defense of these same principles, the price being loss of freedom, unemployment, poverty, persecution, exile from one's country, your decision was a great personal joy and a gift ... the honor which was thus granted to me is shared by all prisoners of conscience in the Soviet Union and in other eastern European countries as well as by all those who fight for their liberation.

Despite these brave words, however, it was not a foregone conclusion that human rights would make the Kremlin susceptible to pressure. Stalin had shown no regard for the concept and, in 1989, the Chinese were to brush such rights under the carpet in Tiananmen Square. So why should it matter to Brezhnev and his colleagues if they were attacked by the West for the lack of freedoms or if a few individuals succeeded in voicing their opposition to the Soviet system on an international stage. The principle that what happened within a country's borders was the affair of that country still remained generally accepted. Even the CIA, in the late 1970s, did not believe that human rights would pose a serious threat to the Soviet Union although it recognised the possibility that the Kremlin might have a different perception.[5] Russian history and Leninist ideology impelled Russians to 'exaggerate the potential importance of opposing groups, however small', CIA analysts reported. The Kremlin was accustomed to being in total control.

History and ideology apart, there were three main reasons why the Kremlin perceived the advocacy of human rights by the West to be a threat to its empire. The first was the threat of internal revolt; the second was the threat of revolt within one or more of the satellite states which might then also spread to the Soviet Union; and the third was the more amorphous possibility that the free exchange of ideas and people, as envisaged by Helsinki, would create, if not a revolution, at least an erosion of communist ideology.

In 1975, when the Russians signed up, they took a 'calculated risk' that this action would not create serious internal difficulties. By 1977, the situation had changed. Unrest had grown in Eastern Europe. The ranks of the dissidents had been swelled by those who were being denied the right to emigrate from the Soviet Union and satellite states. These included Jews who wished to go to Israel and other religious and ethnic groups. In one case, the whole congregation from a Pentecostal church in the south of Russia had applied for exit permits. The case of potential émigrés also became a high-profile campaign. An East German official was reported as saying: 'After Helsinki, they think they can go anywhere they like'. Discontent was further stimulated by a period of poor harvests in the Soviet Union. Moscow feared that food shortages would unite the workers with the human rights dissidents.

In addition, the Kremlin was concerned that the free movement of people and ideas would open society to a host of ideas and influences from the West that were 'not only politically subversive but socially disruptive and morally unhealthy'. Soviet citizens were being exposed not only to 'alien political ideas but also to crime, terrorism, pornography, and drugs, which could combine to produce a general breakdown of order and discipline'.[6]

Attempts to control the dissident problem through a combination of coercive and conciliatory measures were unsuccessful.

Repression was certainly an option and, post-Helsinki, many Soviet dissidents found that their situation had worsened. However, repression alone no longer solved the problem for the Russians. Persecution of high profile figures tended to swell the ranks of the dissident movement. The situation was further complicated by events in Russia's satellite states where movements for change were much stronger. Poland was of particular concern. Soviet authorities were 'alert to the danger of a political "virus" from eastern Europe spreading into the polyglot borderlands of the Soviet Union', the CIA reported.

The Carter initiative on human rights appears to have left Moscow bewildered and confused. The Russians found it difficult to interpret his motives. To what extent was the policy an attempt to bolster his position domestically rather than an attempt to undermine the Soviet Union? Whatever the motivation, it became increasingly apparent to the Kremlin that the Carter policy was having a devastating effect behind the Iron Curtain. The CIA recorded the view that 'the human rights issue was seen by the Soviets as more damaging to Soviet–US relations than the Vietnam war had been, because "then you were bombing Hanoi, but now you are bombing Moscow"'. Nevertheless, the Kremlin remained confident that in the long run it could control the situation. Historical inevitability remained the central tenet of the communist faith. For Russian leaders, steeped in the belief that communism would triumph, failure was not an issue. It was only a question of time.

Solidarity and the Polish Pope

The eruption came, as Moscow feared, in Poland. Two major developments occurred which rocked the foundations of the communist state and from which it was never to recover. These developments were intertwined in a manner which was unique to Poland. The first was the election of the Polish Pope in 1978. The second was the birth of Solidarity in 1980. The momentous nature of these events was rooted in the deep relationship between the Polish national soul and the Catholic Church, a relationship which was steeped in history and which had been given new impetus by the one thousandth anniversary of the Polish nation and the millennium of Christianity in Poland in 1966.[7] The regime feared the powerful passions that Christian symbols and events aroused in the citizens of Poland.

These passions can be seen in what is known as the Lublin Miracle. In 1949, a likeness of the Virgin Mary displayed in Lublin Cathedral was seen to be weeping. Within days thousands of people had flocked to the church from all over Poland where they prayed and wept. The authorities tried to stop the pilgrims by banning the sale of rail tickets to Lublin and putting up roadblocks. They also organised demonstrations against the miracle with people carrying banners saying such things as 'Down with the Clergy' or 'Ignorance and Illiteracy'. The security service reported 2500 anti-miracle rallies in two days alone. The miracle hysteria culminated in a clash between demonstrators carrying red flags and believers carrying crosses. The miracle had become a political issue and the collective memory of it survived well into the 1980s. The first large anniversary was held in Lublin in 1981, at the height of Solidarity's legal existence.

It is no surprise, therefore, that the election of Cardinal Karol Wojtyla of Krakow as Pope set alarm bells ringing in Warsaw. A British diplomat remarked that the Polish government reacted to the news with 'stunned silence'.[8] Having little option, it then affected to greet the event with joy. Pope John Paul II was the first non-Italian Pope since 1522. Church bells rang as the people of Poland greeted the election with uncontained joy, attending religious Masses and demonstrating their enthusiasm on the streets. One commentator remarked that 'the entire country was standing and talking'. It reinvigorated Polish Catholics. For them, it demonstrated that, after more than thirty years of the communist regime and its propaganda, the Church in Poland was still so strong that its cardinal had been elected to lead the global Church. The Polish Pope meant the existence of an external and independent power, supporting the Catholic vision of Poland.[9]

The first major challenge to the Polish government came with the Pope's visit to his homeland in 1979, a year after his election. The whole of Poland was in a state of 'emotional excitement'.[10] It was estimated that the crowds who greeted the Pope numbered about twelve million in total. Both Catholic officials and the government under Edward Gierek, known as a man who believed in compromise rather than confrontation, feared public disorder and what might result from it. They successfully co-operated in trying to preserve stability. Nevertheless, as one observer commented: 'Whatever the long-term consequences of the visit, it has been made clear it is the Church, not the Party, which commands the allegiance of the people in "People's Poland".'[11] Observers also predicted that economic problems in Poland could soon cause renewed instability.[12]

That prediction was realised the following year when Solidarity was founded in Gdansk. Led by a charismatic shipyard electrician, Lech Wałęsa, the union was the offspring of strikes that started in the shipyards and within weeks had spread throughout Poland. The strikers' demands were political as well as economic. They wanted not only better working conditions but also greater freedoms such as a reduction in censorship and, significantly, the broadcasting of a Catholic Mass on Sundays. The main demand was that free, independent non-party trade unions should be allowed and that Solidarity should be given legal recognition. Strike committees were organised at factories throughout the country and links were established with dissident intellectuals. The union turned itself into a mass movement which increasingly began to look like an opposition political party in a one party state. As the movement gathered momentum, Gierek's government seemed to capitulate. At the end of August 1980, an agreement was signed between Solidarity and the authorities, with Wałęsa famously using a pen decorated with a portrait of John Paul II, a souvenir of the papal visit. In effect, for the first time it appeared that a communist regime had legitimised another political organisation. The event was likened to the October Revolution in importance. According to one observer, it was 'the beginning of a workers' revolution against a "Workers' State"'.[13]

The elation was short lived. Promises were made and broken. Only days after the signing ceremony, Gierek was replaced by a new man, Stanislaw Kania. The wording of the agreement turned out to be ambiguous. In October the government unilaterally inserted a clause into the union's constitution asserting the supremacy of the communist party. This point had been the nub of days of wrangling. Solidarity's eight million members were angry. Wałęsa described the new clause as 'a violation of the freedom and independence of trade unions'.[14] It was feared that it would be used to place the union, once again, under party control. A national strike was threatened. The government warned of outside intervention. The forces of the Warsaw Pact gathered on the Polish border. Unrest continued throughout the country. Arrests were made. In November, Solidarity demanded reform of the secret police and threatened more strike action.

The fear that Poland was in the process of its own version of the Prague Spring was keenly felt by the Kremlin and even more so by other members of the Warsaw Pact such as East Germany. Soviet Foreign Minister Andrei Gromyko is reported to have commented: 'We simply cannot and must not lose Poland.'[15] Fearing invasion, Solidarity leaders, counselled by dissident intellectuals and Church leaders, were at pains to stress their moderation and denied that one of their aims was to overthrow the communist government. Warsaw Pact military exercises were held, which put troops in readiness should they be required. The Polish Defence Minister, Woyciech Jaruzelski, claimed that he was asked to agree to the entry of troops into Poland on 8 December. But the Polish government succeeded in convincing the Russians that it would be better to give them time to deal with the situation themselves and that it was able to do so. 'Even if angels entered Poland they would be treated as bloodthirsty vampires,' the Russians were told. The invasion was halted at the eleventh hour.

> **General Jaruzelski** was put on trial in Poland in 2008 charged with using force to crush the Solidarity revolution. He has admitted that he struck a deal with the Russians but claims that he did so in order to prevent an invasion and save bloodshed. Martial law was a lesser evil than Warsaw Pact tanks on the streets of Poland, Jaruzelski claims. The case against Jaruzelski is that the establishment of the Military Council which imposed martial law was illegal even within a communist state.

In January 1981, Wałęsa flew to Rome to be blessed by the Pope. In the Polish countryside, peasants and farmers greeted the new year by forming their own version of Solidarity. A municipal building in a town near the Soviet border was occupied and draped with a banner demanding the registration of a rural Solidarity. The stage was decorated with images of the Pope, an icon of the Virgin Mary known as the Black Madonna and the national flag – that potent mix of symbols. The bust of Lenin they replaced was consigned to a dusty corner backstage.[16]

Later that year, Jaruzelski became party leader and the long-awaited clampdown began. Martial law was declared on

13 December 1981 and continued until the end of 1982. Wałęsa and other Solidarity leaders were arrested. The Party had won – for the time being – but the dam had been breached and communist leaders in Poland and the rest of the Soviet bloc slept less easily in their beds.

It had long been Moscow's fear that 'the lid could blow' in Poland. The CIA reported that the country had the hallmark of a 'revolutionary situation'. The economy was fragile, the army unreliable, the population hostile and, most importantly, there was 'an assertive working class whose interests are defended by two other elements – the Church and the intellectuals'.[17] A puzzling question is why the Russians did not invade Poland and put an end to the Solidarity movement before it got out of control. Had the Brezhnev Doctrine ceased to exist several years before the eventual collapse of communism in Europe? Western observers could not be sure. The doctrine had declared that it was not only the right but also the duty of a communist state to intervene in the affairs of a neighbour if it was thought that communism in that country was under threat. The communist regime in Poland was certainly under threat but the final decision to send in the Warsaw Pact troops could have been merely pre-empted by the imposition of martial law.

One theory is that, faced with the huge domestic problems of economic stagnation and internal dissent, the Russians decided to put their own interests first. East European crises were increasingly seen as threats to Soviet resources.[18] The Brezhnev Doctrine probably did die in Poland in 1981 but its demise was not announced until much later. In addition, there was the human rights issue. The pressure of international human rights made communist leaders hesitate to crush the dissidents and reformers. The USA was moving towards a harder line. Détente was on the wane. A Polish invasion could have signalled its end. Martial law in Poland held the line for a while but the Solidarity movement was only silenced, not broken. It was at this point that a new man took the helm in Moscow. It was the influence of Gorbachev, many say, which was crucial to the ending of the Cold War. Poland aside, the events of 1989 would not have taken place without the Gorbachev factor.

The Gorbachev factor and the end of the Cold War in Europe

How much difference did Gorbachev make to the ending of the Cold War? To what extent was the personality of this man a factor in the disintegration of the Soviet empire? Who was this man who may have changed the world?

The CIA thought he looked rather like the film star Rod Steiger and was a pleasant change from some of his predecessors.[19] It reported that 'Westerners used to the dour demeanour that often characterises Soviet politicians are particularly struck by his expressive face, sense of humour, and ready smile'. On the other hand, the CIA also noted the comment from one of Gorbachev's colleagues that 'this man has a nice smile, but he's got iron teeth'. He was a cultured man, fond of the theatre and the ballet. He was also Russia's first leader from the new generation, too young to have suffered personally from the Stalinist era, a man who apparently took 'motoring holidays' in France and Italy, a man whose lifestyle seemed more capitalist than red. Gorbachev's main aim on taking power was reform. The Soviet Union was stagnating. 'We cannot remain a major power in world affairs unless we put our domestic house in order,' Gorbachev told the party Central Committee in 1984.

Recent trends in historiography have tended to favour great causes as explanations for events rather than great people. It is argued, for example, that it was economic factors which forced the Soviet Union to its knees. But if that were the case, others counter, how was it that Stalin faced much harsher conditions at the end of the Second World War, yet refused to compromise. Cold War historians have put forward a multiplicity of reasons to explain why it was that the Soviet empire crumbled and the Cold War ended. The list of factors responsible for the demise of the Soviet Union include Gorbachev's right-wing reforms; internal stresses inherited from Stalin; the inability of the Kremlin to use force to repress dissent; economic chaos; the growth of technology and the information revolution; and the tough policies of US President Ronald Reagan.

America's role in the ending of the Cold War, and specifically the role of Reagan's policies, is also hotly debated. In 1980, the Americans elected a President who had a deep personal belief that the Soviet Union and communism presented a major threat to US security. Reagan quickly set about changing the tone of US foreign policy. Out went the policy of détente and in came a more hostile and distrustful approach to dealing with the Russians. In 1983, Reagan made his notorious 'evil empire' speech. Committing himself to defending Christianity, he spoke about finding 'peace through strength', argued against a weapons freeze and warned his audience of Christian evangelicals not to 'ignore the facts of history and the aggressive impulses of an evil empire, to simply call the arms race a giant misunderstanding and thereby remove yourself from the struggle between right and wrong and good and evil'. A few days later, Reagan introduced his plan for protecting America from the Soviet threat – the Strategic Defense Initiative (SDI), popularly known as Star Wars. The early Reagan years were a period of deterioration in US–Soviet relations. The USA stepped up its backing for Marxist opposition groups around the world, such as the Contra rebels in Nicaragua. The Russians pulled out of the Los Angeles Olympic Games in 1984.

Nevertheless, around 1984, a shift in Reagan's attitudes towards the Soviet Union is discernible. This was brought about, to a certain extent, by a realisation that the Russians felt threatened by the Americans and that this situation could potentially lead to the nuclear strike that America so feared.[20] A gradual rapprochement began again between the two sides, with meetings taking place between Reagan and Gorbachev and agreement being reached. It seemed as though, once again, the West was moving towards living with the Soviet Union. In the words of Margaret Thatcher, it 'could do business' with Gorbachev.

Regardless of the machinations of the two superpowers and their leaders, throughout the rest of Eastern Europe the cracks were growing deeper. The citizens of the Soviet bloc were taking matters into their own hands. In Poland there was uproar when a popular activist priest linked to Solidarity, Jerzy Popieluszko, was murdered in 1984, reportedly by the secret police. In 1985, there were Solidarity-led boycotts of elections, and 1988 saw a further wave of strikes throughout the country. In Hungary, Karoly Grosz, known as a reformer, succeeded János Kádár as party leader and replaced the old guard on the central committee. The lifting of restrictions on political parties was promised and in October 1989, the communist party reformed itself as a social democratic party. In Czechoslovakia, leading dissidents demanded the release of human rights activist Václav Havel in January 1989. And in East Germany, the people decided that if they could not change the GDR, they would leave it. Taking advantage of less secure borders and lax visa requirements, thousands packed their bags for holidays in Hungary and crossed the border into Austria. Thousands more took to the streets of Leipzig, Dresden and East Berlin, demanding reforms, basic rights and freedoms.

In the midst of this chaos, Gorbachev visited East Berlin in October 1989 to join in the fortieth anniversary celebrations of the GDR. People joked that in 2009 the GDR would be sixty and would therefore be able to travel west legally – as pensioners were entitled to do.[21] In fact, it was only a matter of weeks before the joke became reality. Gorbachev cold-shouldered the beleaguered East German leader Honecker during the so-called celebrations. Honecker was a rigid hardline old-fashioned communist, out of step with the times and an irritation to Gorbachev with his reforming agenda. In 1971 when Ulbricht had been pushed from power, Honecker had been Moscow's man but by 1989 he was its man no longer. Other members of the GDR politburo saw which way the wind was blowing during a meeting with the Soviet leader over the weekend of the anniversary celebrations. Whereas Gorbachev talked of the problems the countries of the Soviet bloc were facing, Honecker merely repeated his mantra about the successes of the GDR. He appeared blind to the demonstrations taking place across East Germany. Gorbachev is reported to have told Honecker's colleagues that life would punish those who delayed. Only two weeks after Gorbachev's visit to the East German capital, Honecker was gone, replaced by Egon Krenz who was more willing to follow Gorbachev's line.

A few days after the visit, a Soviet spokesman told the world that Russia now favoured the Sinatra Doctrine rather than the Brezhnev Doctrine, a reference to the song 'My Way'. In effect, the Kremlin washed its hands of its unruly protégés. They were now free to make their own decisions and solve their own problems.

As the GDR's neighbours set about dismantling their one party states, the East Germans set about pulling down their wall. On 9 November 1989, at a press conference in East Berlin, politburo member Günter Schabowski announced that new travel regulations would allow all GDR citizens to apply for visas to travel west. When asked when these changes would take place, he incautiously replied 'immediately'. The word spread like wildfire. Thousands gathered at the Berlin Wall. The border guards, under pressure and seemingly without any clear instructions, simply opened the barrier and the people poured through. Thus did the Cold War in Europe effectively end – almost by accident.

During the years of détente, the West had invested heavily in building up channels of communication with Eastern bloc countries and promoting human rights. The dividend was paid in the final years of the 1980s when the protests of Soviet bloc citizens reached a crescendo. The protestors were responding to the message that had been emanating from the West since the Helsinki agreements; the message that championed basic human rights for all, including those who lived behind the Iron Curtain. The Russian fear that Helsinki would erode communist ideology proved justified. What has perhaps not always been realised in the West is the fact that this 'erosion' was a political strategy deliberately designed by Western politicians in order to bring about the defeat of communism.

But the dissident movement alone would not have enabled the quiet revolutions of 1989 to take place. Another ingredient in the political mix was needed if the tanks were not to roll in as they had done in previous decades. It was the combination of the human rights movement with the Soviet Union's decision to let its unruly satellites sort out their own problems that enabled the Iron Curtain to fade away. The death of the Brezhnev Doctrine in the early 1980s was one of the most significant events of the later Cold War. Yet it passed almost unnoticed at the time. If the doctrine had still been a key plank of Soviet policy in the late 1980s, Hungary, Poland, Czechoslovakia and the GDR would not have been able to quietly slip from Russia's grip as they did. If the Russians and other Soviet bloc leaders had still been convinced of the need and indeed duty to fight to protect communism, then the East European upheavals of 1989 would have resulted in enormous bloodshed. The Soviet Empire might still have collapsed but it would not have done so relatively peacefully as it did.

The Cold War left its imprint across the globe. In some regions its impact has been more lasting than in Europe where the conflict began. For countries in Asia, Africa, Latin America and the Middle East, struggling to assert their independence following the end of the Second World War, the ideological conflict which followed was an ingredient which served to curdle an already unstable mixture.

6

Cuba and Latin America

The fear of the world being obliterated by a nuclear explosion was as real to most Britons during the middle years of the Cold War as the fear of German invasion during the Second World War. People lived under the 'black shadow of the mushroom clouds', the historian Eric Hobsbawm has recalled. 'We were all living in a kind of nervous hysteria.'[1] Small boys were known to have leafed forward to future exercises in their algebra books pencilling in 'Are we at war yet?' The government issued civil defence advice on how to survive a nuclear attack. Farmers were told what they could do to make their farms safer from radioactive fall-out. The screening of a film about the effects of a nuclear attack on Britain was banned by the BBC in 1966 because it was thought to be too horrifying.[2] This fear of nuclear holocaust was shared by millions around the world. The moment when it appeared most probable that the fear could become a reality was during the Cuban missile crisis when Russia and America faced each other down in the Caribbean. For thirteen days in 1962, it is commonly said that the world held its breath. In the event disaster was averted. But the aftermath of Cuba coloured the Cold War for the remainder of its duration and continues to affect US–Cuban relations in the twenty-first century.

There were both positive and negative aspects to the Cuban crisis. Having come so close to the abyss, political leaders in Moscow and Washington became more cautious. There was a reaction against creating a situation in which the wriggle room for the other side was so small that nuclear weapons seemed the only option. The period of détente which followed the Cuban missile crisis was partly a product of that event. On the other hand, Cuba heightened tensions between Washington and its Caribbean and Latin American neighbours, and had a deep and lasting impact on US relations with the region. Successive US presidents became hypersensitive to suspicions, however ill-founded, that communism might gain even a toehold in their backyard. They had little compunction in interfering in the affairs of other nations in the region, both covertly and overtly. The history of the Cold War in the Caribbean and Latin America is largely the story of US interventionism; of coups, guerrilla wars, dirty tricks and invasions. At the same time, Washington exaggerated the Soviet threat throughout the Cold War, that strategy reaching 'absurd' levels during the Reagan years.[3]

Cuba – a colossal mistake[4]

On 16 October 1962, Kennedy was alerted to the fact that US spy planes had spotted Soviet nuclear missiles on Cuba, a mere 90 miles or so off the Florida coast. The weapons were capable of striking virtually every city in the USA. They had been secretly placed there by Khrushchev in response to a plea for help from the island's revolutionary leader, Fidel Castro, who feared a second US-backed invasion was imminent. The news was an enormous shock for the young, recently elected President. For the first time, Americans were vulnerable to nuclear attack from Soviet missiles. Kennedy was also personally angered by what he saw as Khrushchev's duplicity. The two men had a secret channel of communication through a Russian intelligence officer called Georgi Bolshakov. Kennedy had been assured by Khrushchev that the Soviet Union would not rock the President's domestic political boat and would not deploy offensive weapons on Cuba.

Kennedy was faced with a dilemma. American hardliners were already accusing him of being soft on communism. Firm action was essential for domestic political reasons. His first move was to set up a crisis committee which became known as the ExComm.

The Executive Committee of the National Security Council, generally known as **Excomm,** was a small group of advisers drawn from different areas of expertise who advised President Kennedy during the Cuban Missile Crisis. These men held the future of the world in their hands. The group was able to defuse the crisis and it is now regarded as a successful model for the resolution of international crises. Members of Excomm included President Kennedy's brother and US Attorney General Robert, Secretary of Defense Robert McNamara, Secretary of State Dean Rusk, National Security Adviser McGeorge Bundy, and General Maxwell Taylor, Chairman of the Joint Chiefs of Staff. There were also representatives from the CIA and other agencies. The group totalled twenty-three but there was an inner circle which met more frequently. The meetings were secretly recorded by President Kennedy and the tapes are now available at the John F. Kennedy Library. They have also been transcribed. The recordings have enabled historians to analyse in remarkable and unusual detail the way in which the Kennedy administration handled the crisis.

The two options on the table were an airstrike to take out the missiles, or invasion. Kennedy judged an airstrike to be too risky. No one was sure if the missiles were operational or how many there were. There was no guarantee that an airstrike would destroy all the missiles before the Russians and Cubans could retaliate. The chances of an invasion being successful also seemed slim and the use of force could spread to Europe, at the very least provoking a Soviet takeover of Berlin, that most vulnerable of Cold War cities.

Importantly, Kennedy had decided to keep the discovery of the missiles secret for as long as possible until he had decided what to do. For several days, the Russians were not aware that their secret missiles were secret no longer. The American public did not know that Soviet nuclear missiles were targeted on their homes. Kennedy and the ExComm were able to talk through the options for six vital days in a relatively calm and rational atmosphere while, all the time, US spy planes brought home more information about the nature of the threat.

Kennedy favoured a naval blockade. American ships would form a cordon around Cuba and any ships heading for the island which were found to contain offensive weapons would be turned back. The advantage of this plan was that it would give Khrushchev time to negotiate. He would not have to respond to an attack with its dangers of nuclear retaliation. A disadvantage was that under international law a blockade was an act of war and therefore it could be said that the USA had declared war on the Soviet Union. The Americans got round this by calling the blockade a 'quarantine'. On 22 October, Kennedy went on television to tell the world about the missiles and the blockade.

Meanwhile, Khrushchev had begun to suspect that something was afoot in Washington. He was receiving reports of increased US military activity and learned of Kennedy's planned broadcast a few hours before it took place. Fearing the worst, the Kremlin prepared for an attack. America's NATO allies, also alerted to the danger, looked on with alarm. The threat of Soviet nuclear missiles was nothing new to Western Europe which had been within range for some years. Its fear was that Kennedy might overreact to the situation. Khrushchev was not alone in his relief that Kennedy had given the Russians some breathing space. The Soviet leader responded cautiously. Soviet ships on their way to Cuba were ordered to turn back. US Secretary of State Dean Rusk famously commented on hearing the news: 'We're eyeball to eyeball, and I think the other fellow just blinked.' There would be no confrontation.

Such was the tension between the two sides, however, that both Kennedy and Khrushchev continued to fear that the situation could escalate out of control and war could begin accidentally. One wrong move, one jittery soldier or sailor firing against orders and the result could be a nuclear explosion. Both men therefore trod carefully. Kennedy chose to allow two ships, carrying innocent cargoes, through the blockade to give Khrushchev more time. Both men secretly negotiated through their back channels while making bellicose public statements. Khrushchev told Kennedy that he would remove the missiles if America promised not to invade Cuba. Kennedy told Khrushchev that he was prepared to negotiate and would lift the blockade if Khrushchev removed the missiles. The two sides reached agreement on 28 October. The UN stepped in to act as mediator.

What was not made public at the time was another part to the deal. Kennedy also agreed to remove US missiles from Turkey, close to the Soviet border, but only on condition that that part of the pact was kept secret. If the truth had become known in America, it would have been political suicide for Kennedy. Khrushchev agreed to the secrecy clause. The Cuban crisis had provided him with the leverage that he needed to force Kennedy to remove the Turkish missiles. This side of the affair was strenuously denied by the Americans at the time but of late it has been suggested that the main purpose behind the Cuban nuclear deployment was to provide Russia with a bargaining counter to push for the removal of weapons threatening her territory. The two issues, Cuba and Turkey, were connected in British minds even as the crisis was intensifying. *The Times* judged:

Amid it all, the chief hope ... after Russia has made the obvious *riposte* to the charge that a missile base so near to America is a threat to peace. What about American missile bases on Russia's frontier? ... there is just enough similarity in the siting of some of the bases to cause the question to be raised ... it is just possible ... that they may consider a bargain whereby each does away with a forward base or two. With a ban on nuclear testing added, the world's nerves could become steadier.

Kennedy stuck by his secret deal and the Turkish missiles were scrapped or removed by April 1963. The part they had played in the Cuban crisis remained a secret for twenty years.

At the time of the crisis, Khrushchev's decision to deploy missiles in Cuba was portrayed in the West as another act of communist aggression. It was a 'Soviet challenge in an American sphere of vital influence'. But the story has, until recently, been largely told from the American point of view; at the time in a book by Robert Kennedy, the President's brother, and as recently as 2000 in a film of events based on tapes of Kennedy's crisis meetings.[5] The Russians saw the crisis as a local issue, in that it was justifiable action to defend Cuba against US aggression, and also as a possible winning move in the global Cold War. The Cubans had their own agenda but their role and their demands were lost in the struggle between the two giants and have, until recently, been largely ignored.

Fidel Castro came to power in Cuba in 1959 following a guerrilla war against the right-wing dictator Fulgencio Batistá. Relations between the USA and Cuba had been poor since 1898 when the Americans defeated Cuba's colonial master Spain in the Spanish–American War and took control of the island. For the next sixty years, Cuba was dominated by her large and powerful neighbour. Some Americans hoped, and many Cubans feared, that Cuba would be swallowed up by the USA. Although most American troops withdrew from the island shortly after the Spanish defeat and it was agreed that Cubans should govern themselves, the island was effectively a US protectorate until 1959. The Americans retained a naval base at Guantánamo Bay – a situation which became a bone of contention during the missile crisis. One of Castro's main demands in return for his co-operation in resolving the crisis was that the Americans should return the base to Cuba. But the Americans refused and the Russians were not prepared to dig their heels in on this issue

Castro's assumption of power and attempts to reduce American economic influence on Cuba led to Eisenhower breaking off relations with Cuba in 1960. Until this point, Castro's communist connections had been low key. He was a nationalist and a revolutionary; not, at that point, a committed communist. But US hostility pushed him gradually into the arms of the Soviets – despite the fact that the Russians were initially not sure if they wanted to welcome this romantic and unpredictable figure into their camp. The event which sealed Cuba's fate was Washington's disastrous decision to orchestrate an invasion of the island and oust Castro.

CIA-trained Cuban exiles landed at the Bay of Pigs in 1961 with the aim of overthrowing the revolution. The plan was drawn up under Eisenhower and inherited by Kennedy. The invasion was a shambles and most of the invaders were taken prisoner by Cuban forces. The affair served only to increase American animosity towards Castro and plans for a second attack were soon under way. Washington claimed that its aim was to 'help the people of Cuba overthrow the Communist regime from within Cuba and institute a new government with which the United States can live at peace'.[6]

Castro, aware of the US invasion plans and Cuban vulnerability, turned to the Soviet Union. He needed help but actively opposed the idea of deploying nuclear weapons on the island. In his view conventional weapons would have been sufficient deterrent against a US-backed invasion. Indeed, Castro believed that simply making public a Cuban–Soviet defence pact would probably have provided adequate protection.

Khrushchev, it seems, was playing a Cold War power game. Just like Kennedy, he was under pressure from his own hard-liners. He calculated that by deploying nuclear missiles on Cuba he could achieve several objectives at once. He could protect Cuba from American invasion; demonstrate Soviet missile strength; show the world that it was Russia not China which stood strongly against capitalist aggression in support of small nations; provide himself with a bargaining counter to bring about the removal of the Turkish missiles; and possibly strengthen his hand in Berlin. He also made the mistake of reckoning that Kennedy was weak and unlikely to react. What about putting a hedgehog down Kennedy's trousers, Khrushchev is reported to have said to one of his advisers.[7]

Whereas for both Kennedy and Khrushchev, the Cuban missile crisis was a tactical skirmish within the Cold War conflict, for Castro it was a serious local matter, evolving out of a history of troubled relations between Cuba and the USA. He was furious when Khrushchev appeared to back down and complicated the US–Soviet agreement by refusing to allow UN officials to carry out weapons inspections. Cuba was an example, of which there were many, of the superpowers failing to comprehend the passions generated by a small nation's desire for post-colonial independence.

Thirteen months later, Kennedy was dead. One of the biggest questions to come out of the Cuban missile crisis, and indeed one of the biggest questions of the Cold War, is who was behind his assassination. Despite the protestations of the Warren Committee which investigated the killing and judged that there was no conspiracy, theories continue to abound. Some have argued that Castro was behind the killing; others that the American Mafia, which was deeply involved in Cuba, organised the shooting in Dallas. But recently released documents showing that Kennedy was seeking an accommodation with Castro in 1963 and was preparing for a secret meeting with the Cuban leader suggest that Castro had little motive to kill Kennedy at this point.[8] What part, if any, did the secret plans for a US rapprochement with Cuba play in Kennedy's death? The question has been asked as to whether Kennedy was the real victim of the Cuban missile crisis.[9]

Intervention in Latin America and the Caribbean

The Bay of Pigs invasion had not been America's first adventure in the region. That honour was claimed by Guatemala in 1954 when the CIA helped to bring down the elected government of Jacobo Arbenz. Arbenz advocated social reforms. He was not a communist but legalised the communist party in the country and allowed it to operate freely. One of his major flaws, in American eyes, was to introduce land reforms which threatened American agricultural interests and through the American prism smacked of socialism. When Czech arms were delivered to Guatemala in May 1954, the CIA claimed this was proof of Russian intervention. 'The real purpose of the Communists is to secure for the imperialistic movement of Russia the complete subservience of the peoples of the Western world, and the resources therefrom', read a CIA report on the situation.[10] Following an invasion by US-trained troops under Castillo Armas, Arbenz was deposed and replaced by Armas.

The impact of the Guatemalan coup was threefold. Firstly it provided Washington with a blueprint for future interventions in the region. Secondly it intensified anti-American feeling within Latin America. And thirdly it established a US pattern of supporting right-wing dictators in Latin America.

The Dominican Republic was next to feel the power of the USA. The first elected government had been overthrown in 1963 and a civil war was raging. US troops were sent to the island in April 1965 to support military leaders against those fighting for a return to the constitution and the reinstatement of the previously elected president, Juan Bosch. Washington feared that if Bosch regained power he would be indebted to left-wing and communist supporters. At one point, 23,000 US troops were deployed on the island. Evidence now suggests that US fears were unfounded. The Soviet Union was not involved and Cuba only slightly so. It was an example, one historian has noted recently, of the USA deploying 'massive force to ward off a threat that did not exist'.[11]

In September 1970, Chile elected a socialist president, Salvador Allende. Nixon's reaction was that Allende was 'not acceptable' to the USA and he ordered the CIA to 'prevent Allende from coming to power or to unseat him'.[12] Washington had a fear of the domino effect taking place in Latin America, just as it had feared would happen in Asia.

There is a clever party trick whereby you stand some dominos up, one behind the other, spaced at regular intervals and knock the first one over. If you have it right, this will start a chain reaction resulting in all the dominos neatly falling one after the other.

This simple idea was the basis for American foreign policy during the Cold War. The theory stated that it was necessary for the USA to prevent communism taking hold in small countries far removed from its own shores because, if it did not, the neighbouring countries would also fall to communism, as would their neighbours and so on until communism reached America's own borders. The domino theory, as it is known, was the predominant reason for US intervention in Vietnam, and subsequently in a host of other countries in Africa, the Middle East and Latin America.

President Eisenhower first used the expression in April 1954 when asked a question about the importance of Indochina to the USA. A few weeks later, the CIA helped to depose the socialist president of Guatemala, the first direct intervention by the USA since the end of the Second World War. Presidents Kennedy, Johnson and Nixon were also wedded to the idea of the domino theory. They claimed that the chain reaction that would result from Vietnam becoming a communist state would stretch around the world starting with Laos, Cambodia, Burma, Thailand, Malaya, India and Japan then moving on to Australia, Africa, Latin America and, finally, Europe.

The domino theory provided the USA with a justification for intervening in any part of the globe. As a political theory, however, it has been shown to lack intellectual rigour. It presupposes the existence of an aggressor state seeking world domination and that smaller states are closely tied to the aggressor state. It also makes the assumption that political events are irreversible, which is not the case. What the domino theory did not allow for was the fact that frequently revolutions, coups, civil wars and internal conflicts take place within countries for reasons indigenous to them. During the Cold War, the root cause of many conflicts was nationalism and a desire for independence from any other imperialistic power whether that be Russia, China or the USA.[13]

Kissinger advised Nixon that:

The example of a successful elected Marxist government in Chile would surely have an impact on – and even precedent value for – other parts of the world, especially in Italy; the imitative spread of similar phenomena elsewhere would in turn significantly affect the world balance and our own position in it.[14]

It was three years, however, before Allende was toppled in a military coup backed by Washington and replaced by the

right-wing dictator Augusto Pinochet.[15] Once again, the extent
of Soviet involvement in Chile and the reality of the threat of a
communist bridgehead on the South American mainland remain
open to question. According to some historians, it was slight –
'the Soviet–Chilean relationship could hardly justify US
policies'.[16] Others consider it to have been more real, recording
that both the KGB and the CIA made strenuous efforts to
control Chile.[17]

The pattern repeated itself in Nicaragua in the 1980s. The
country had been effectively ruled by one family, the Somozas,
since the 1930s with Anastasio Somoza in power from 1967.
Although he had been supported by the USA, his reactionary
and brutal rule led Carter increasingly to stand on the sidelines
as opposition within the country gained momentum. Somoza
was ousted in 1980 by guerrilla fighters known as the Sandinista
Liberation Front. The ruling group, led by the Marxist Daniel
Ortega who had received guerrilla training in Cuba, was made
up of nationalists, revolutionaries and communists. They
preached revolution throughout the region, particularly in
nearby El Salvador where guerrillas were fighting a brutal right-
wing regime.

Although Ortega looked to Russia and the Soviet bloc for
support, they reacted cautiously. Ortega's revolutionary rhetoric
was out of step with the Kremlin's views on Third World
revolution at that time. It was only after much pleading from
Nicaraguan revolutionary leaders that the Soviet Union eventually agreed to supply weapons, most of them coming via third
countries such as Cuba and Algeria.

With Reagan in the White House, the administration's
opposition to Ortega intensified. Nicaragua and El Salvador
became places where Washington's increasingly proactive
policies against global communism could be prosecuted.
America was responsible for training, equipping and funding a
15,000-strong counter-revolutionary force in Nicaragua known

as the Contras. This intervention spilled over into El Salvador where the Reagan administration helped to prop up the regime. In 1983, however, the administration's Central American policy suffered a setback when the US Congress cut off American funding for anti-communist forces in the region. Critics alleged that the USA was giving its support to undemocratic and murderous regimes and feared that the USA might be drawn into another Vietnam. They claimed that the administration's 'blinkered determination' to see the upheavals in the region in Cold War terms blinded it to the real problems of social, political and economic injustice.[18]

Three years later though, the tangled and murky world of covert US action against Nicaragua exploded onto the world stage in the shape of the Iran–Contra Affair. It was revealed that members of the Reagan administration had been selling weapons to Iran, contrary to US policy, and secretly using the proceeds to buy weapons for the Contras. The scheme was investigated by a Senate committee, the Tower Commission, which produced a report critical of Reagan and led to the prosecution of some of the administration's security advisers.[19] The affair continues to reverberate around the corridors of power in Washington. The fighting in Nicaragua left around 30,000 dead. In neighbouring El Salvador, 70,000 were killed.

The Reagan administration had judged that they had a green light for a more aggressive policy against Central American revolutions following the US invasion of the small Caribbean island of Grenada in 1983. Although it was condemned by friend and foe alike, the reaction from the Soviet Union was muted, indicating that the Russians were no longer prepared to make grandiose gestures to defend infant revolutionary regimes as they had done in Cuba. 'Grenada showed that it could be done ... it proved that boldness and determination could defeat the Communists,' one member of the Reagan administration has been quoted as saying.[20]

Viewed from Washington, Grenada, a former British colony and member of the Commonwealth, was another dangerous breeding ground for Cuban-style revolutionaries and Soviet influence. The trouble began when the socialist Prime Minister, Maurice Bishop, was deposed and killed following a split in the People's Revolutionary Government which had seized power four years earlier. Ironically it was thought that Bishop was not Marxist enough for some of his colleagues. They were critical of his recent attempts to establish better relations with the USA despite the fact that he had been rebuffed by Washington. Following Bishop's death, Reagan went on television to tell the American people: 'Grenada bears the Soviet and Cuban trademark, which means it will attempt to spread the virus among its neighbours.'[21]

A few days later, America shocked the world by invading Grenada. The island's tiny population of fewer than 100,000 was quickly overwhelmed by the US invasion force of 6000 men backed by 15 warships. Washington claimed that it acted in response to a plea from the Organisation of East Caribbean States. Grenada was not a friendly island paradise for tourism as Grenadians claimed, Reagan said. 'It was a Soviet–Cuban colony, being readied as a major military bastion to export terror and undermine democracy. We got there just in time.' *The Times* suspected that Reagan, unable to make any visible headway in his struggle against communism in other countries in the region, found the idea of a quick military victory against a small island appealing.

The British government's opposition to the invasion of Grenada, where the Queen was head of state, fell on deaf ears. One letter-writer to *The Times* asked: 'Is there any part of the world that is not America's backyard?'[22] The invasion was condemned in the UN and by Washington's European allies as well as most Latin American countries. Subsequently, seventeen former members of the Grenadian government and armed services were sentenced to imprisonment for the rest of their lives. In 2003, the human rights organisation Amnesty International issued a report describing them as 'the last of the Cold War prisoners'. In 2007, British law lords ruled that the trials of the men had been 'politically charged' and they should be resentenced by a Grenadian court, thus leading to their eventual release.

While Washington saw Soviet influence behind every Latin American revolutionary leader, the Kremlin's elderly and conservative leaders were more circumspect. Cuba apart, Latin America was never high on the Soviet foreign policy agenda.[23] The Kremlin was wary of the hotheads far away from Moscow's controlling hand who preached a different sort of socialism. The initiative for Soviet involvement usually came from the Latin American side rather than the other way round with Castro frequently leading the way, dragging the Russians behind him. Any ambitions that had been entertained in Moscow for Latin American revolution faded following Cuba and the onset of détente.

After America's Vietnamese humiliation, the idea of supporting emerging nations against US economic and military imperialism saw a resurgence in the Kremlin but, even so, the support provided in Latin America was limited for economic and logistical reasons. In addition, by the start of the 1980s, the Soviet Union was bogged down in its own war of intervention in Afghanistan. Soviet interventionist capabilities lagged behind those of the USA for the rest of the Cold War.

During the Cold War, Washington under different administrations deemed that it had the right to interfere in other countries. Nowhere can this be seen more clearly than in Latin America. Time and again, American troops and American clandestine agents moved in on the governments of independent countries in order to protect the USA from what was perceived to be a communist threat that might take hold in America's backyard. The Cuban missile crisis had rubbed at a raw nerve in the American psyche which never healed despite the fact that it was only in Cuba that serious Soviet involvement in the strategically distant countries of Latin America was evident. From 1962 onwards, the words 'another Cuba' were enough to strike fear in the minds of all Americans and justified the excesses of interference. But Washington's determination to stamp out anything with the smell of socialism in the Latin American region was not brought about because of the Cuban missile crisis. The policy was there from the outset, as could be seen in Guatemala in 1954 and the Bay of Pigs invasion of Cuba in 1961. In 1977, when President Carter, attempting to introduce a more ethical foreign policy, spoke about the manner in which the USA had adopted the flawed and erroneous principles and tactics of its adversaries and abandoned her own values for theirs, thoughts turned to American support for unelected right-wing dictators in Latin America.

The region's Cold War differed from that of other areas of the world in that Washington was fighting spectres. The reality was that there was little serious opposition to the USA from either Russia or China in that area. Bloody battles in the name of capitalism or communism were much more dangerous to the peace of the world in Asia, for example, where both sides clashed head on. It was in Asia that the two great military wars of the Cold War took place – the Korean War and the Vietnam War.

7

Asia

If communism was to sweep across the globe in the early Cold War years, as Marxism predicted and the West feared, then Asia seemed a likely starting point. Viewed from across the Pacific, the countries of the Orient appeared uniquely vulnerable to the red peril. During the first decade of the Cold War, China, Korea, Vietnam, Cambodia, Laos, Indonesia, the Philippines and Malaya all turned to communism or were the scene of violent confrontations with communist forces. In many cases, the communist rebels had fought against Japanese occupation during the Second World War and continued the struggle for independence against returning colonial rulers. In contrast to the Middle East where political ideology was a flimsy garment to be donned or discarded at will, in Asia tens of thousands died in bloody wars in the name of communism.

Three events of great significance took place in this region during the first thirty years of the Cold War. China, the world's most populous country, became a communist people's republic. A civil war in Korea dragged the USA, the Soviet Union, China and their acolytes to the brink of a third world war. And in Vietnam, another civil war bloodied the American nose to such an extent that the nation's psyche is still scarred by the humiliation and trauma.

As in other parts of the world, the two great colonisers were Britain and France. French colonies included Vietnam, Cambodia and Laos, all scenes of conflict. British colonies included Malaya, India and Burma, the latter two achieving independence in 1947 and 1948. A 'jungle war' against communist guerrillas was fought in Malaya for ten years. The Dutch were the colonial masters of Indonesia until independence in 1949. Following the coup which brought Suharto to power in 1967, hundreds of thousands died in an 'orgy of violence', many of them communist or left-wing sympathisers.[1] Soviet interest focused on those countries which bordered its territory, such as China and Korea. Russian priorities were to protect her eastern flank and also obtain access to warm water ports, a major long-term goal for a country whose long Arctic coastline was frozen for much of the year. America was the relative newcomer on the scene.

China awakes

The slumbering giant of the East was China. In 1949, the communist leader Mao Zedong took control of the country following a civil war against the nationalists or *Kuomintang*. Both the Soviet Union and the West were unsure how to react to the changed circumstances. It seemed as though Stalin had gained an important ally but his enthusiasm for Chinese communism was tempered by his fear of Mao as a rival. The defeated nationalists set up a power base on the offshore island of Taiwan and claimed to be the legitimate government of the whole of China. In the unreal world of the Cold War, the USA and many other countries went along with this fiction. The USA did not officially recognise the communist government in Beijing until 1979. The British, pragmatic as ever, quickly accommodated themselves to the new situation and recognised the People's Republic of China in 1950, a move which displeased Washington.

It was Russia's relations with China, however, which were probably of most significance to the course of the Cold War. The fact that by 1949 two of the largest countries in the world were staunchly communist appeared to shift the balance-of-power away from the West. But the relationship between Russia and China was rarely smooth and during the middle years of the Cold War was so bad that a rift developed which became known as the Sino-Soviet split.

There were a number of factors that made relations between the two countries difficult but chief among them was a difference in ideology. The Chinese were the purists, aiming to harness the revolutionary spirit of the people to create a utopian form of communism, first in their own country and then around the world. The Russians leaned towards political realism. *The Times* wondered whether Khrushchev could hint to the Chinese that a little less ideology and a little more attention to the facts of the outside world might be more fruitful. Mao was also attempting to bring the economy into the industrialised twenti-eth century. The project, known as the Great Leap Forward, was an economic disaster.

Nevertheless, Mao persisted in his belief that it was the revolutionary spirit of the people rather than the bureaucrats of the Soviet model that would make China a truly communist nation. This political philosophy was seen again during the Cultural Revolution between 1965 and 1968. The Chinese people were exhorted to return to the basic principles of the revolutionary movement and condemn the liberal tendencies Khrushchev had introduced into the communist world. Maoism became an international cult. The leader's revolutionary thoughts appeared in the *Little Red Book*, which replaced Marx as the new communist bible. Thousands took to the streets waving their copies in the air, not only in China but also in the West where many post-war baby boomers were relishing the idea of revolution.

Moscow and Washington both looked on in alarm as China rocked the status quo. Indeed, during the 1960s, the Russians feared that China rather than the USA was the greatest threat to world peace. The Chinese, for their part, accused the

Mao Zedong set China on the road to becoming a great world power again. In 1949, with the defeat of the ruling nationalist party, the Kuomintang, he united China as it had not been united for centuries. Born in Hunan province in 1893, he was the son of a relatively wealthy peasant. He believed that human will could conquer all obstacles. He also believed in the emancipation of women. Mao dated his Marxist beliefs from the time of the first translation of the Communist Manifesto into Chinese in the early 1920s. In 1921, he was one of the founding members of the Chinese Communist Party. One of the turning points in Mao's career was known as the Long March. The Chinese communists had split with the Kuomintang, led by Chiang Kai-shek. Mao decided to set up a communist region in north-west China, protected by mountains. About 100,000 men and their families set out on the 8000 miles march in 1934. About a third of them reached their destination about twelve months later. The Long March became a patriotic legend in Chinese communist history. During the Second World War, the communists and nationalists united against the invading Japanese but civil war had resumed by 1948. Mao was formally elected communist leader in 1945 and, following the defeat of Chiang Kai-shek, became Chairman of the People's Republic of China in 1949. Mao believed in the power of persuasion rather than force and set about uniting the country. He also believed in the powerful interaction of the masses and revolutionary leaders, the one drawing strength and commitment from the other. His slogan was 'from the masses, to the masses'. The Great Leap Forward in 1958 was an attempt to increase the speed of collectivisation among the largely peasant population, reinvigorate their revolutionary zeal and, by diverting the peasants away from the land and into industrial processes, modernise the economy. The plan was an economic failure due to natural disasters, disastrous harvests and gross mismanagement. Millions starved to death. The Chinese reverted to more orthodox forms of development. Nevertheless, Mao's ideas were revered across the world, particularly in under-developed countries, and his revolutionary strategy was copied by many. He died in 1976.

Soviet Union of counter-revolution.[2] They objected to the
Soviet policy of détente. Peaceful co-existence in the eyes
of Maoist ideologists looked like an abandonment of
Marxism–Leninism. The Chinese believed that communism
would triumph only through violent struggle. Hostility between
the two countries was so great that in 1969 Russian and Chinese
troops clashed over disputed territory on China's northern
border.

The conflict between the two great communist states was
studied intently in Western capitals despite a lack of hard information about the inner thoughts of the Chinese and Russian
leaders. Western leaders looked to using the Sino–Soviet split to
their own advantage. In 1960, for example, the British observed
that:

> It is too early to say whether it will necessarily be to our advan-
> tage to try to aggravate any divergence which may one day
> appear between the policies of China and Russia: it is conceiv-
> able that, at any given time, we might wish to see the restrain-
> ing influence of Russia prevailing in Peking or, even
> conversely, the more subtle and flexible policy of Russia
> hamstrung by Chinese intransigence.[3]

Later, Nixon and Kissinger played on Sino-Soviet rivalry to
bring about a realignment of Cold War power blocs.

The schism between Russia and China was felt in the two
major wars that were fought in Asia – the Korean War of
1950 to 1953, and the Vietnam War of 1965 to 1973. From
Washington's perspective, both were fought against communist
expansionism. In reality they were a complex mix of civil
war, post-colonial struggle for independence and a jockeying
for position in the communist world by Russia and
China.

The Korean War

Korea's troubled Cold War history began at Yalta in 1945. The country had been annexed by Japan in the early part of the twentieth century. Following Japanese defeat in the Second World War, Korea was divided into two parts, the northern sector occupied by the Soviet Union and the southern by the USA, pending ultimate unification. This arrangement, which maintained stability, came to an end in 1947 with the withdrawal of occupying troops. In 1948, elections were held. The right-wing nationalist leader in the south, Syngman Rhee, was declared the ruler of the whole of Korea after the communist leader in the north, Kim Il Sung, refused to participate. Kim promptly proclaimed the north to be the independent Korean People's Democratic Republic. For the next two years both sides engaged in skirmishes across the 38th parallel, which had been arbitrarily decreed to be the border between the two sides.

Both Washington and Moscow exercised a restraining hand on their warring protégés. Stalin's preferred scenario was that Korea should eventually be united under Kim not through invasion but through a revolutionary movement in the south. He wanted to avoid the Soviet Union being dragged into a war that he judged the North Koreans would not win. The Americans did not at first see Korea as being of great strategic importance. They were more concerned about other developments in the region in the early part of 1950, particularly Vietnam where the French were losing the battle against the communist north and the government of Ho Chi Minh had been recognised by both Russia and China. US Secretary of State Dean Acheson announced that the USA had excluded Korea from what it called its 'defense perimeter'.

The question that has exercised historians over the years is what made Stalin and Truman change their minds about the importance of Korea, seemingly within a matter of weeks. For, in 1950, Stalin approved Kim's plan to take the southern part of Korea by force, and troops from the USA and other nations went to the aid of the south. For the next three years a ferocious battle raged back and forth on the peninsula threatening to destroy the peace of the world.

The picture presented to the American people at the time was that the invasion was a Soviet controlled move, a part of the communist world revolution. In Washington, where McCarthyism was on the rise, Korea was put forward as proof of the threat of the red peril. But it has since become evident from communist archives that the initiative for the invasion came from Kim, not Stalin. Only months earlier Stalin had had to back down in Berlin over the blockade. Another trial of strength had not been on his agenda. His motives for changing his mind were rather more cunning than world revolution.

Stalin thought he could see a way of achieving two of his objectives at the same time by allowing Kim to proceed with his invasion plans. First, if Kim was successful, Stalin could gain access to the warm water port of Pusan in the south of Korea. This would replace the Chinese warm water port which he had lost at the beginning of 1950 when Russia and China had signed a new so-called friendship treaty. Second, if the invasion ran into trouble, Stalin planned to make the Chinese pick up the pieces. He manipulated the situation so that Mao was obliged to commit China to the North Korean invasion. Kim was told that if America intervened, which Stalin doubted it would, then Kim must turn to China for help, not the Soviet Union. 'If you should get kicked in the teeth, I shall not lift a finger. You have to ask Mao for all the help,' Stalin is reported to have told Kim.[4] Stalin also judged that if China was involved in a Korean war, she would be prevented from attacking Taiwan. The Russians did not see it as being in their interests for the Chinese to strengthen their position in the region by taking this breakaway island off the Chinese coast which claimed to be the legitimate government of China.

Mao had been reluctant to encourage Kim's bellicose plans, mainly because he was fully occupied with domestic matters but also because the priority for the Chinese in the area was Taiwan, not Korea. However, he was left with little option. Mao had been promoting himself as the true supporter of nationalist revolutionaries around the world and could not afford to be seen to be failing to back such a close neighbour.

The North Korean invasion took the south by surprise and swept all before it. Within three days, Kim's army had captured Seoul. The USA, contrary to Russian expectations, reacted swiftly, sending in troops and mobilising support at the UN. Despite Acheson's earlier speech, Washington had in fact decided to take a tough stance against anything that smacked of communist expansion.

Unknown to the Kremlin, Washington had drawn up a new strategy for fighting the Cold War. Its essence was contained in the policy document NSC 68 which committed the USA to fighting the spread of communism, wherever that may be and by military means if necessary. Washington's problem was to sell this to the war-weary American people, to persuade them that it was necessary to spend a huge amount of their taxes on weapons to fight this battle.[5] In this context, the start of the Korean War was a godsend for the White House. Here was the perfect example of the threat that Truman and his colleagues needed to prove their point.

Initially, the war went well for the North Koreans. After taking Seoul, they pressed south defeating the poorly equipped and outnumbered Americans. By September, North Korea occupied almost the whole of the Korean peninsula. At this point the tide turned. UN reinforcements arrived and forced the North Koreans to flee. US and UN troops followed them across the 38th parallel and took the North Korean capital.

The US Commander-in-Chief, General Douglas MacArthur, then made the mistake of continuing his advance north to the Chinese border. Mao, under threat, sent in his own troops which forced a UN–US retreat. By January 1951, the Chinese and North Koreans were back south of Seoul again. MacArthur wanted to take the war onto Chinese territory. He even advocated the use of atomic weapons, a proposition which horrified America's allies. Just as the Russians feared letting China off the leash, so Britain feared that America was the greatest danger in Asia.[6] Under pressure, in April 1951, Truman stepped back from the brink and dismissed MacArthur. 'We do not want to see the conflict in Korea extended. We are trying to prevent a world war – not to start one,' he told Americans.[7] The war drifted into stalemate along the 38th parallel and finally ended in 1953 when the UN brokered a ceasefire. Korea remained divided. Never again, Americans vowed.

The Vietnam War: an error of judgement

The Vietnam War has probably had more words written about it than any other single event in the Cold War. It has been the subject of histories, novels, films and music and has been examined in minute detail from multiple angles.[8] Remembered popularly in the West as America's bloody fight against communism in Asia, the eight-year war that ended in 1973 was actually a continuation of two other wars – the post-Second World War battle to expel French colonialists and the civil war into which that struggle developed. The Vietnam War divided the world, alienated the USA's allies and scarred Americans for decades to come. It is estimated that about 58,000 Americans and more than six times as many Vietnamese lost their lives. The destruction was huge. During one three-year period, more bombs were dropped on North Vietnam than had been dropped on Europe during the whole of the Second World War.[9]

The debate about why the war took place has been fuelled by the invasion of Iraq which is frequently likened to Vietnam because of the manner in which a foreign power can become bogged down in essentially regional or national issues which it does not understand. The ability to see the war from different perspectives has been made possible since the end of the Cold War by the availability of limited access to Vietnamese, Russian and Chinese archives. More nuanced questions have been raised about the motives and objectives of all the countries involved, including the USA. The current view is that American ignorance in the 1960s about Vietnamese history and culture helped to create a distorted analysis of the situation.[10] Guerrilla leaders such as Ho Chi Minh had been fighting for independence since the days of Japanese occupation during the Second World War. The fighting continued when the French tried to reimpose colonial rule. Washington was unable to differentiate between the struggle for national liberation from foreign powers of any nationality and the threat of communist expansion.

Ho Chi Minh, the North Vietnamese revolutionary leader, was one of the iconic figures of the communist world. He was a living link between Lenin and Brezhnev having joined the Communist Party shortly after the Russian Revolution. He lived in Moscow during the 1920s and knew Lenin personally. He was also a hero to young anti-Vietnam War activists in the 1960s. During demonstrations, the chant of Ho, Ho, Ho Chi Minh was a rallying cry for young protestors on the streets of Western cities. Ho Chi Minh was born Nguyen Tat Thanh in 1890 in Vietnam, at that time a French colony. He was to use many aliases, adopting the name Ho in the 1940s. He learned French at school, became a teacher and then signed on as a steward on a French liner which enabled him to travel the world. In London during the First World War he worked in the kitchens of the Carlton Hotel. In 1918, he settled in Paris. When the French Communist Party was formed in 1920, Ho became a founder member. After studying in Moscow, he moved on to China where he founded the Vietnamese Revolutionary Youth League. He was unable to return to Vietnam because, as a known revolutionary, he would have been arrested by the French. In 1931, the British arrested him in Hong Kong and charged him with sedition. One of those who defended him was Stafford Cripps, later to become Chancellor of the Exchequer in the Attlee government. During the Second World War, Vietnam was occupied by the Japanese. Ho joined Vietnamese exiles in China and formed a communist movement which became known as the Viet Minh. The organisation was armed and supported by the US wartime intelligence agency, the OSS, in order to help drive the Japanese out of Vietnam. With their defeat, Ho declared a Democratic Republic of Vietnam. For the next eight years he fought a bitter war of independence against the French. *The Times* recorded in his obituary in 1969 that in manner and dress he resembled Gandhi but that his mild exterior concealed a shrewd, calculating and ruthless political brain. 'With the death of Ho Chi Minh the communist world has lost a man who will rank alongside Lenin, Stalin, and Mao Tsetung as one of the outstanding figures of the movement.' Ho was not only a communist and a nationalist. He also sought the liberation of all non-white people from their white dominators.

The French had been finally defeated at Dien Bien Phu in 1954. Later that year, at a conference in Geneva, Britain, France, the USA, the Soviet Union and China agreed that Vietnam should be partitioned. The communist Democratic Republic of Vietnam in the north was led by Ho Chi Minh. The anti-communist Republic of Vietnam in the south was headed by the US-backed Ngo Dinh Diem, who had spent many years in exile in America. Fighting between the two halves of the country continued with the south being infiltrated by the northern backed Front for the Liberation of South Vietnam, known as the Viet Cong.

As the situation in the south worsened, the newly elected Kennedy decided to increase US aid to South Vietnam. Washington feared the domino effect in Asia, believing that if South Vietnam fell to the communists, other countries such as Laos, Cambodia and even Thailand, Malaya and Indonesia would topple too. However, the problem for Kennedy was that Diem was not the man to win the allegiance of the South Vietnamese and create a strong and stable nation state. He was part of the problem rather than the solution, alienated from the population by his Catholic faith in a predominantly Buddhist country and by his years in exile. His corrupt and repressive methods, especially against the Buddhist population, was a breeding ground for the Viet Cong. Buddhist monks burned themselves alive in Saigon in protest at Diem's dictatorial behaviour. He was finally deposed during a military coup in October of that year and murdered a few days later.

US complicity in the coup and the murder was investigated by the Church Committee in 1975, which concluded that the USA had encouraged the coup but had not been involved in the assassination.[11] Washington strengthened its commitment to the new government in South Vietnam. The north meanwhile judged that the assassination increased the chances of US military involvement and therefore stepped up its support for the south with the aim of winning the battle and pre-empting further intervention.

With Kennedy's murder following only a few days after that of Diem, it was Johnson who faced the problem of what to do next: withdraw and leave Saigon to the North Vietnamese, or stay and fight. He chose the latter. For domestic political reasons he could not be seen to be soft on communism. Washington failed to realise that it was involving itself in a regional civil war.

The USA needed a pretext for attacking North Vietnam. That was provided by the Gulf of Tonkin incident in 1964. A

US destroyer probing North Vietnamese coastal defences was attacked by three Vietnamese patrol boats. Both sides opened fire. It was the first time the USA had engaged the Vietnamese directly. The following day the US navy reported a second torpedo attack on the destroyer, which had been ordered back into the area. The claim was retracted within hours. It was said that it had been a mistake, a false alarm, caused by bad weather and poor communication systems. Nevertheless, Johnson immediately launched an airstrike on North Vietnam – in retaliation, he claimed. America was effectively at war. Suspicions about the veracity of the Tonkin affair were aired as early as 1967 by some Congressmen who alleged that the Tonkin episode was deliberately provocative, designed to engineer America's entry into the war.[12] In 2005, The US National Security Agency released secret documents relating to the incident. It is generally agreed that the second attack never took place.[13] But it served its purpose and by the following year, there were 400,000 American troops in Vietnam.

Up until this point the Kremlin had been trying to restrain the North Vietnamese, urging a negotiated settlement. After Tonkin, it saw little alternative other than to provide support for the north against what was seen as imperialist aggression. The number of US troops in Vietnam continued to rise. Young Americans were drafted into the armed forces in their thousands. Anti-Vietnam War protests took place across America and around the world.[14]

America's attempts to bludgeon the North Vietnamese into submission with massive air power seemed to be working as the decade progressed. But in January 1968, the north launched an attack known as the Tet Offensive in a last ditch attempt to capture the initiative. The move took the battle deep into US-held territory. Pictures of fierce fighting in Saigon were beamed around the world. It was a public relations disaster for America despite the fact that the offensive is generally regarded as a defeat for the Viet Cong. Calls for an end to the war multiplied as anti-Vietnam protesters joined forces with civil rights activists and left-wing revolutionaries on American streets. Johnson, coming to the end of his presidency, decided it was time to negotiate. The war had become unwinnable.

With the election of Nixon in 1968, the US aim became a gradual withdrawal of troops and a handover to the South Vietnamese. The problem was to achieve this without giving the appearance to the world that America had been defeated. The warring parties were persuaded to the negotiating table on several occasions, often under pressure from their supposed allies, but it was not until January 1973 that a peace deal was finally signed. The Paris Peace Accords left Vietnam a divided nation. South Vietnam remained an independent state. Fighting between north and south continued and two years later Saigon fell to the communist north. A unified Socialist Republic of Vietnam was declared in 1976.

The generally held view of the Vietnam War is that it was an enormous error of judgement by the Americans.[15] They had convinced themselves that they were the guardians of freedom and democracy, the world needed to be protected, and they alone were in the position to do this. They failed to take into account several facts: neither the Soviet Union nor China was actively promoting a North Vietnamese military attack on the south; the country was not of great strategic importance; the costs of protecting limited American interests were high; and the strongest motivating force for the Vietnamese was not Marx but self-determination. The Americans persuaded themselves they were fighting Soviet and Chinese expansionism when in fact they were involving themselves in a post-colonial revolutionary movement. 'It was never clear', one historian has written, 'how the dropping of bombs on the followers of Ho Chi Minh would nurture democracy without alienating millions of Vietnamese.'[16] US Secretary of Defense during the Vietnam War, Robert

McNamara, has recorded that a North Vietnamese foreign ministry official told him many years later:

> Never before did the people of Vietnam, from top to bottom, unite as they did during the years that the US was bombing us. Never before had Chairman Ho Chi Minh's appeal – that there is nothing more precious than freedom and independence – gone straight to the hearts and minds of the Vietnamese people as at the end of 1966.[17]

America's allies were reluctant to be involved. British experience of fighting communist guerrillas during the Malayan Emergency could have been useful for the Americans but, despite seeing herself as America's closest ally, Britain chose to remain neutral. The Vietnam War was an 'all-American show', a British Foreign Office official wrote in December 1963 as military escalation began following Kennedy's death.[18] As the fighting intensified, the pressure on Prime Minister Harold Wilson to send troops increased but he stuck to his role as an honest broker.

There are three factors to be taken into consideration in relation to the Russian view of the Vietnam War. First, the conflict took place during a period of great rivalry between China and Russia, culminating in the Sino-Soviet split. Second, Russia was more concerned about events in Europe, such as the Prague Spring in 1968, than in fighting wars in Asia. And third, the Kremlin had deemed that a policy of détente, or peaceful co-existence, would serve Soviet purposes better at that time.

Initially, the Russians doubted that the North Vietnamese could win the war and saw it as an obstacle to détente. Ho's decision to support armed rebellion in South Vietnam was taken against Russian and Chinese advice.[19] The Kremlin's attitude shifted following the reversal of communist fortunes in

Indonesia, and as the possibility of a North Vietnamese military victory became more likely. Mao, on the other hand, wanted to support Ho but the domestic situation in China was so bad following the Great Leap Forward that he was not in a position to offer much help. Nor did Mao want a war with the USA on his doorstep.

However, once the war was underway, Mao increased his support. It served his purpose to present China as being threatened by capitalist forces. As is often the way, a threat to the state, whether real or perceived, increased national cohesion and strengthened the role of the leader.[20] In addition, the more relations deteriorated between Russia and China, the more Mao pledged his support for North Vietnam. He wanted the world to see that it was China, not Russia, which was the true promoter of revolutionary movements.

Nevertheless, Mao was only in favour of a limited expansion of the war. Following Tonkin, China issued some bellicose anti-American statements, but the rhetoric was largely for domestic consumption or intended as a verbal shot across the American bows. Chinese aid largely took the form of defending strategic areas within North Vietnam and undertaking engineering works. Brotherly love between the Chinese and the Vietnamese became strained as the war progressed and when the Vietnamese agreed to begin peace negotiations in 1969, the Chinese withdrew their support. By this time, Hanoi had further alienated the Chinese by flirting with Moscow again. The dispute between the two communist powers was so bitter that it prevented them from uniting against America. Indeed, by late 1968 China was beginning to countenance the idea of talking with Washington, and in 1971 Kissinger had secret talks in Beijing to prepare the ground for Nixon's visit the following year.

The Vietnam War led directly into one of the greatest policy shifts of the Cold War: rapprochement between the USA and

China. Nixon and Kissinger set out to play off the Soviet Union against China, a policy which was known as triangular diplomacy. The Chinese, wary of the Russians and looking for economic growth, were prepared to accept American advances. The rapprochement resulted in China becoming a key strategic partner of the USA during the latter years of the Cold War.

It was in Asia that the commitment to communist ideology was most strong. It was in Asia that thousands were prepared to die for the cause. And it is in Asia where communism continues to survive most strongly both in the form adopted by the Chinese, and in the closed society of North Korea. Washington's attempts to suppress communism in the region failed despite the fact that it was prepared to go to war twice in order to defeat the perceived threat. Nevertheless communism did not infect the whole region, as Washington claimed it would. In the post–Cold War world Asia is the region where communism and capitalism co-exist most successfully.

8

The Middle East

The echoes of the Cold War in the Middle East have continued to reverberate around the world. The history of those years was arguably more complex than in any other region of the world. The global division between communism and capitalism was shrugged off by Middle Eastern leaders who played the Cold War game by different rules. For them, the Iron Curtain was more of a beaded screen; constantly shifting, brushed aside at whim, and almost impossible to control.

While Washington and, to a lesser extent, Moscow viewed the Middle East through the distorting prism of the Cold War, Middle Eastern countries focused on their ancient rivalries and feuds, and on asserting their national identities.[1] Regional leaders had no ideological commitment to either superpower. Their aim was to steer a course between them. If they made alliances, they were based on calculations of what could be gained. Allegiances could change overnight. Coups, rebellions and political assassinations were the order of the day, making uncertainty the key element of international relations.

But the Middle Eastern struggle to remain aloof from the Cold War was as hopeless as trying to hold back the tide. Inexorably, the region was pulled into the mesh, trapped in the logic that decreed if you are not with us, you are against us. It was a logic that was frequently self-fulfilling. The nuances of Middle Eastern politics were largely lost on Americans who came newly to the region and saw only a strategically vital area in their own conflict. The Soviet Union, more practised in the art of Middle Eastern politics, helped itself to the spoils which came its way, often as the result of US blunders.

There were three particular factors which differentiated the Middle East from other regions of the world. One was the presence of oil. Large reserves in countries such as Iraq, Iran and Saudi Arabia were always a consideration in the decision-making processes of the oil-thirsty superpowers. The second factor was the Arab–Israeli conflict. The whole period was punctuated by brief wars and sporadic skirmishes between Israel and her Arab neighbours, particularly Egypt. In the context of the Cold War, this had a destabilising effect but was not central to the global struggle. America and the Soviet Union acted either as cheerleaders or referees, the former on behalf of the Israelis and the latter for the Arabs. The third factor was the rise of a new political force based around the predominant religion of the area. Islamism rejected both communism and capitalism as political models and became the enemy of both. The simple Cold War logic of East versus West, which was difficult to apply to secular Middle Eastern leaders, became even less valid with the rise of Islamism.

The Middle East is a region with a recorded history that stretches back many thousands of years. The countries contained within it have experienced over the centuries domination by Greeks, Romans, Turks and Arabs, among others. It is an area with no rigid borders. The term 'Middle East' is a loose description, coined by the British, of the area that lies at the juncture of Europe, Africa and Asia and includes countries such as Egypt, Iran, Iraq, Israel, Syria, Turkey, Saudi Arabia and small states in the Arabian Gulf. For the purposes of this chapter, it also includes Afghanistan and the countries of North Africa. Its geographical situation has made it strategically important and also influential in world affairs over many centuries. It is home to great civilisations which have provided a basis for global erudition.

Three of the major Cold War players had a history of occupation and colonisation in the region. The Soviet Union shared common borders with Iran, Turkey and Afghanistan, and both Britain and France had colonised the area. Iran and Iraq were occupied by the British and the Russians during the Second World War and Britain had a large military presence in Egypt into the 1950s. The French had colonised the Maghreb, the Arabic name for the northern part of Africa bordering the Mediterranean. They were also influential in Egypt, French engineers having built the Suez Canal. The USA had no history of involvement but the presence of oil soon attracted its attention. From the perspective of the major Cold War players, the Middle East was the second front of the conflict after Europe because history and oil dictated that the two sides operate at close quarters.[2]

Conflicts and crises

The first Arab–Israeli war took place in 1948, following the end of the British mandate. Syrian, Egyptian, Jordanian, Lebanese and Iraqi troops invaded Israel but were repulsed. The war ended in 1949, with Israel extending her territory and feeding the resentment of her Arab neighbours. Throughout the 1950s and 1960s, there were sporadic skirmishes between Israel and Egypt and her allies, the most significant being the Six Day War during the summer of 1967. Again Israel was the victor. The Yom Kippur War of 1973 brought Russia and America to the brink but the principle of superpower détente dictated that they drew back. These conflicts created the background against which the Cold War in the Middle East was acted out.

The Suez Crisis of 1956 was the first major Cold War conflict. Suez was instrumental in creating a world dominated by two superpowers. Britain and France were humiliated and demoted to the second division as their colonies seized the moment to assert their independence; the USA replaced Britain and France as the dominant Western power in the region and Egypt was pushed into the arms of the Russians.

The immediate cause of the crisis was the nationalisation of the canal by Gamal Abdel Nasser, President of Egypt, on 26 July 1956. Britain and France, the two major shareholders in the Suez Canal Company, saw this action as a threat to their interests. Together with Israel they secretly prepared to invade Egypt. It was agreed that Israel should launch an attack on Egypt which Britain and France would use as a pretext for intervening and taking possession of the canal. The invasion provoked a chorus of condemnation from around the world, led by the USA which had not been consulted. Washington demanded that the UN call for a ceasefire. The pressure was so great that Britain and France were forced to withdraw within days. US opposition was compounded by the fact that the invasion took place at exactly the moment that Russian tanks were rolling into Hungary to quell the uprising. For the Hungarians the Suez Crisis was a disaster. With the world's gaze focused on the Middle East, Khrushchev effectively had a free hand to crush the revolt.

France was under additional pressure at the time of Suez because she was heavily engaged in a colonial war in Algeria. This was probably the first conflict in which terrorism was exported to the country seen as the oppressor. The Algerian War of Independence began in November 1954 and continued for the next eight years, during the course of which the French government fell and Charles de Gaulle, the wartime saviour, returned from retirement to rule France. The Algerian war was a brutal guerrilla conflict with the wave of violence spreading to mainland France and the neighbouring French colonies of Morocco and Tunisia.

The victors in the Suez Crisis were Nasser and the Soviet Union. Nasser, an army officer, had seized power in 1952 following a military coup in which the pro-British monarch

The **Algerian War of Independence** is remembered for its brutality, its terrorist atrocities and its use of torture as an instrument of interrogation by both the French and the Algerians. The French saw Algeria as being a part of France. About one third of its population was white. The conflict was complicated by the fact that rather than being a clear-cut battle between a colonial power and an independence movement it was a three-way fight which also involved extreme right-wing French nationalists determined to ensure that Algeria remained French. The revolutionary FLN (*Front de Libération Nationale*) was led by Ahmed Ben Bella and fought in the name of Arab nationalism. It received support from Nasser. In 1956, the French hijacked a plane carrying Ben Bella, contrary to international law, and imprisoned him in France for five years without trial. The OAS (*Organisation Armée Secrèt*) was a right-wing terrorist group led by senior French army officers who turned on their own government when it sought an accommodation with the FLN. In 1958, the Fourth Republic collapsed, besieged by economic turmoil and international criticism of its conduct in the Algerian war. The OAS initially saw de Gaulle as a saviour, the man who would keep Algeria French. But by 1959, as de Gaulle sought to reach a compromise solution based on Algerian self-determination, he came to be seen as the enemy by the OAS. It made several attempts to assassinate the President, including machine-gunning his car. Terrorist atrocities spread to mainland France. The war finally came to an end in 1962 when Algeria was granted independence. Like the Vietnam War, this conflict scarred the French psyche and remains a factor in relations between France and Algeria. A memorial to the many thousands who died in the Algerian war was finally erected in Paris in 2002, forty years after it ended.

King Farouk was forced to abdicate. Nasser's main aim was to establish Egypt as the centre of Arab nationalism. His dislike of colonialist Britain was matched by his wariness of the Soviet Union. His was an authoritarian undemocratic government. He is quoted as saying that he saw no point in establishing a parliament in which men sat serving the interests of London, Washington or Moscow while masquerading as Egyptians.[3]

British and American attempts to manipulate Nasser and keep him in the Western camp backfired. Their methods pushed him towards the welcoming arms of the Russians, a pattern that was to be repeated in the region. When, shortly before the Suez debacle, Britain and America tried to exert pressure on Nasser by reneging on a deal to finance the Aswan Dam, he turned to the Russians. Nasser also found the Russians helpful when the British, Egypt's traditional supplier of arms, attempted to use this situation to control him. When shipments from Britain were restricted, replacements arrived from the Soviet bloc.

Following the withdrawal of Britain and France from Egypt, Washington saw only a power vacuum. American concerns about Egyptian loyalty to the West had been exacerbated in 1955 by Nasser's refusal to join the anti-Soviet alliance known as the Baghdad Pact. This was a British-inspired arrangement backed by the USA, which was intended to be a Middle Eastern form of NATO. Together with the Southeast Asian Treaty Organisation (SEATO), it was designed to complete the ring of containment around the Soviet Union. Iraq, Iran, Pakistan and Turkey were persuaded to join, largely for regional reasons. Nasser chose to stand aloof, along with Syria and Saudi Arabia. America's Cold War analysis of the situation failed to appreciate the nationalistic ambitions of Arab nations such as Egypt and their desire for independence from imperial powers of any political persuasion. Washington saw only the threat of international communism. In 1957, the US President unveiled his new Middle Eastern policy. The Eisenhower Doctrine marked the entry of the USA into Middle Eastern affairs as the dominant player. Eisenhower pledged that the USA would assist any Middle Eastern nation to resist the forces of communism, not only with economic support but also with the use of military force if necessary.[4]

What the Americans did not understand was that US assistance looked more like another imperialist threat to many Arab nationalists. Nor was it realised that Arab leaders, trying to walk a tightrope between Moscow and Washington, would fall into the Soviet camp if it looked like a softer landing. As a result of Suez and the Israeli situation, Egypt was lost to the West until the mid-1970s. Iran and Iraq, historical rivals, both of which were pro-Western at the start of the Cold War, were seen as alternative allies by the West.

Iraq and the rise of Saddam Hussein

Iraq was part of the Ottoman Empire until its collapse in 1918 at the end of the First World War. It then became a British mandate with full independence being achieved in 1930. After the Second World War, under King Feisal II and the Anglophile politician Nuri es-Said, Iraq became a centre for moderation in the Arab world, opposed to the radicalism of Cairo. Both men were murdered during the Iraqi Revolution of 1958, which established a republic under Abdul Karim Qasim with the support of the pan-Arabic Baath Party.[5] During the next twenty years, there was a succession of presidents, some of whom died violent deaths. The country was officially ruled by Ahmad Hassan al-Bakr from 1968 to 1979, but the power behind the throne was a young Baath Party member, Saddam Hussein, who eventually forced Bakr out and took over the presidency.

Like Egypt, Iraq attempted to remain independent in the Cold War both before and after its revolution of 1958. Hostility to the old colonial power, Britain, and its Western ally America was countered by historical fear of the Soviet Union. Iraqi leaders were both anti-imperialist and anti-Marxist. But Said, Qasim and Saddam all used the rhetoric of the Cold War in order to gain economic and military support. For Saddam the challenge was to 'derive material benefits' from the Cold War conflict without 'paying the penalty of abiding by its rules'.[6]

However, American fears of Soviet influence in the Middle East coloured their perception of Iraqi attempts at manipulation, especially as British influence in the region waned and the need for oil grew. As the Middle East moved up the American agenda, the USA became increasingly involved in Iraqi politics. It is thought, for example, that the CIA was involved in the murder of Qasim in 1963, alarmed at his 'flirtations with communism'.[7]

As Saddam Hussein increased his control of Iraq and introduced reforms to modernise the country, the West began to show an interest in him. In 1969, the British Embassy in Baghdad described him as a 'presentable young man' and, in words later famously used by Margaret Thatcher in relation to Gorbachev, one with whom the British government 'could do business'.[8] Saddam, though, continued with his policy of keeping all his options open, signing a Treaty of Friendship with the Russians in 1972. Shortly afterwards he nationalised the Iraq Petroleum Company, which did not endear him to the British, who were the main shareholders.

The USA was slow to adopt Saddam as a Middle Eastern saviour, having broken off diplomatic relations with Iraq in 1967 following the Arab–Israeli war. For a time Iran was America's closest Middle East ally, that tie coming to an end with the Iranian Revolution in 1979. However, the lack of formal ties between Iraq and the USA did not preclude backdoor diplomacy. In 1975, Kissinger met the Iraqi Minister of Foreign Affairs in Paris to press for closer relations between the two countries. The main obstacle for the Iraqis was American support for Israel and Iraq's Kurdish minority, which had been receiving arms from Iran and the USA. Kissinger was conciliatory on both issues. He told the Iraqi minister:

> Our two countries have not had much contact with each other
> in recent years, and I wanted to take this opportunity to estab-
> lish contact. I know we won't solve all our problems in one
> meeting. It will take at least two (laughter) ... Our basic attitude
> is that we do not think that there is a basic clash of national
> interests between Iraq and the United States.[9]

But the factor which served to weld Iraq and the USA together
was the emergence of Iran as a common enemy; the Iranian
Revolution in 1979 and Saddam's decision to go to war with his
neighbour the following year made allies of the USA and Iraq.

Iran and the rise of Islam

Like Iraq, Iran had been occupied by both the British and the
Russians during the Second World War. The Cold War
presented the country with an unwelcome dilemma. The
Russians posed a territorial threat, encouraging a secession
movement in the southern part of Azerbaijan, which belonged
to Iran. The British were an economic threat, controlling
Iranian oil reserves through the Anglo-Iranian Oil Company
(later British Petroleum [BP]) and taking most of the revenue
for themselves. The Shah, who ruled Iran through his prime
minister, was pro-British having been placed on the throne by
the British in 1941. In 1946, the Russians were forced to back
down in Azerbaijan when American pressure was brought to
bear, this crisis frequently being cited as the first skirmish of the
Cold War. Iran looked as though its allegiance was to the West.

But by 1951 there was unrest in the country as nationalist
sentiments grew along with demands that Iran should control its
own oil industry. The prime minister was assassinated, the Shah
forced into a figurehead role, and the government was taken
over by the nationalistic elder statesman Mohammed Mossadeq.

He nationalised the Anglo-Iranian Oil Company. For the next two years the British were instrumental in trying to persuade the Americans that Mossadeq should be removed. For the British it was an economic matter. The Americans, however, saw Mossadeq as politically unreliable. As in Egypt and Iraq, Iranian attempts at neutrality were perceived by the USA as being pro-communist. In 1953, MI6 and the CIA devised a plot to overthrow Mossadeq. Known as Operation Ajax, this is thought to have been the first Western covert operation of the Cold War designed to bring about regime change. A coup was engineered through the use of propaganda, staged demonstrations, bribery and attacks on religious leaders. Pressure was put on the Shah to agree to American demands. The aim was to 'reach an equitable oil settlement' and establish a government which would 'vigorously prosecute the dangerously strong Communist Party'.[10]

The new prime minister, Fazlollah Zahedi, did not last long with the Shah taking control of the country in 1955. For the next twenty-four years, Iran was to be America's closest ally in the Middle East. The change came in 1979 when the Shah was deposed by the Islamic religious leader, Ayatollah Ruholla Khomeini. The Iranian Revolution established an Islamic Republic and introduced another element into the Cold War. Islamism condemned both capitalism and communism. Its legitimacy came from God. 'America plans to destroy us, all of us,' Khomeini told Islamic pilgrims in 1980. 'We have turned our backs on the East and the West, on the Soviet Union and America, in order to run our country ourselves.'[11]

Americans were stunned a few months after the revolution when Iranians took over the US embassy in Tehran and held sixty-six US diplomats and citizens hostage. The action was sparked by an American decision to allow the exiled Shah into the USA for medical treatment. More importantly, Iranians had not forgotten about the CIA's involvement in the overthrow of

Mossadeq and feared a similar plot against the Islamic Republic. A low point in American Cold War history was reached during an abortive rescue attempt in April 1980. The hostages were held until January 1981 when they were released on the day that Reagan took over the presidency from Carter. The Iran hostage crisis was a humiliating disaster for America.

With Iran devoid of support from its powerful superpower ally, Saddam judged that the time was ripe to invade his neighbour and settle some old scores. The Iran–Iraq war, which continued until 1988, was again a regional rather than a Cold War conflict. The two countries epitomised the ideological divisions of the Middle East – Khomeini advocating a fundamental religious state and Saddam representing the secular state. Iran, with a predominantly Shia population, had also been encouraging revolt among the Shias of Iraq. Saddam anticipated a quick victory but initial Iraqi advances into Iranian territory were repelled and by 1982 the tide seemed to have turned.

The USA, professing itself to be neutral but fearing an Iranian victory, openly began to supply Saddam with weapons and mounted a diplomatic initiative to improve US–Iraqi relations. Reagan dispatched a young presidential envoy to Baghdad to smooth the waters between Washington and Baghdad. His name was Donald Rumsfeld, later to become Secretary of Defense under George W. Bush and one of the chief architects of the invasion of Iraq in 2003.[12] The official report of the meeting judged that it 'marked a positive milestone' in US–Iraqi relations and 'would prove to be of wider benefit to US posture in the region'.[13] For his part, Saddam stressed that Iraq still regarded itself as being non-aligned and had no 'ideological complexes'. It was 'unbalanced' for Iraq to have diplomatic relations with the Soviet Union and not with the USA, he told Rumsfeld. The USA needed to 'understand the area better', and take note of Iraqi views so that it did not make mistakes. No country can live in isolation, he said.

Afghanistan and the Mujahedin

The Russians, meanwhile, stood on the sidelines, partly because neither Iran nor Iraq made welcome bedfellows, but mostly because they had problems enough in Afghanistan. Lying on the southern border of the Soviet Union, this was yet another country which had been fought over by Russia and imperial Britain in previous centuries. For much of the Cold War, both the Russians and the Americans had been content to leave the Afghans to their own devices. The country's rulers attempted to remain neutral although inevitably they leaned more towards their powerful neighbour, the Soviet Union. The Americans relied on their powerbase in Iran, another of Afghanistan's neighbours. For them, Afghanistan was a useful buffer state.

That situation changed in 1978 when, following a coup, a communist government took control. The political situation in Afghanistan was chaotic. The Communist Party was deeply divided with intense hostility between the two main factions. The victors in the coup were Nur Mohammad Taraki, who became president, and his second in command, Hafizullah Amin. There is no evidence that the coup was engineered by the Russians but the Kremlin did offer its support to the weak fledgling government.

From the start, the Taraki government faced strong opposition from traditional tribal leaders, Islamists, and rival communists. The Islamist rebels, who became known as the Mujahedin (from the Arabic word for 'struggle'), were provided with a base in neighbouring Pakistan from where they mounted violent attacks on the Taraki government and its Soviet advisers. The Russians were reluctant to provide troops, fearing rightly that they would be drawn into a civil war. They were also suspicious of elements of the Taraki government. Amin, for example, whose brutal brand of communism was too extreme and volatile for the Russians, was suspected of being in contact with the CIA.[14]

The communist coup alarmed the Americans. They feared that the Soviet Union might try to extend its influence in the region through Afghanistan just when the Americans had lost their power base in Iran. That both the Russians and the Americans seemed to be facing the same enemy, Islamism, did nothing to subdue Cold War rhetoric in Washington. Opportunistically, the USA decided to initiate a programme of covert support for the Islamist rebels operating out of Pakistan.[15] Involving itself in this way has had far reaching consequences. But at the time the Americans saw it as an opportunity to undermine the Russians, even though they themselves were being depicted as the devil incarnate in neighbouring Iran.

The situation in Kabul deteriorated when Amin murdered his colleague Taraki and took over the government. Despite Amin's supposedly communist allegiance, the Russians feared that Afghanistan could fall to the West. 'There is no guarantee that Amin, in order to secure his personal power, would not turn to the West,' the head of the KGB advised Brezhnev.[16] Reluctantly, the Russians decided that the only way to solve the Afghan problem was to oust Amin and send in troops. This they did on Christmas Day 1979. Amin was executed and replaced by the head of the opposing communist faction, Barak Karmal, who had always been seen by the Russians as a more amenable leader.

The invasion of Afghanistan was a disaster for the Soviet Union. It is frequently referred to as Russia's Vietnam. For ten years, the Russians were caught up in a fierce guerrilla war which no amount of aerial bombardment could win. It drained Russian resources and aroused hostility to the Soviet Union around the world, particularly among the Islamic people of the region. The question is why the Russians decided to invade Afghanistan, a communist ruled state, the only one in the Middle East throughout the whole of the Cold War. There was strong opposition in the Kremlin. Brezhnev was advised that the move would ruin détente, that Afghans were not ready for socialism, and that it would destabilise the Islamic populations of the Soviet Union. But other voices prevailed. For them, the Russian invasion was a demonstration, the final one as it happened, of the Brezhnev Doctrine; détente was virtually over anyway; socialism would prevail; and, importantly, with the Iranian Revolution Afghanistan had suddenly become a key state in the Soviet area of influence.

The Afghan War was the CIA's largest and 'most successful' covert operation ever.[17] But again the question is asked: why did the USA decided to plough billions of dollars into supporting tribal leaders and Islamist extremists in a mountainous under-developed country that had been deemed of little strategic importance at a time when Islamists were denouncing the USA as the evil enemy? The official view was that Carter feared that the Afghan invasion was the start of a Russian push towards the Indian Ocean. An alternative interpretation of US action is that the Americans funded the Islamist rebels in order to harass the Russians and deliberately suck them into a Vietnam-like situation.[18]

The crisis intensified when Reagan took over in 1980. He advocated a hardline policy against the Russians. Negotiations were not on the agenda. The key to Reagan's policy was Pakistan, which gave the rebels shelter and support. Reagan offered Pakistan economic and military support, which made the country the third largest recipient of foreign aid. All other considerations were swept aside; a veil was drawn over its poor human rights record, its nuclear weapons programme, and its support for the more extreme Islamist groups as Pakistan came to be seen as the supporter of freedom fighters. The tragic futility of the whole exercise has been summed up by one historian who wrote that a combination of 'fear, pride and superpower obligations caused the leader of the "free world" and the "vanguard of Socialism" to struggle violently over a destitute country the size of Texas for the next ten years'.[19]

As the war dragged on, weapons poured into Afghanistan from both sides. Thousands were killed or made homeless. Afghan feuded with Afghan and frequently used their new-found weapons to settle local disputes. For six long years the UN tried to broker a peace deal with little success. The Afghan conflict turned into the biggest proxy war of the Cold War in the 1980s with the CIA providing nearly three billion dollars to the Mujahedin, more than all other CIA operations combined in the decade. In 1986, the USA even provided the Mujahedin with an anti-aircraft missile, the first time that American weapons had been used in a covert operation to support rebel groups. The extent of US aid to the Mujahedin was, in fact, no secret. Financial details were published in *The Times* in 1984 in an article headed 'Afghans Profit from US Double Standards'.

Eventually, the tide turned with the arrival of Gorbachev on the political scene. Once again, the Cold War thawed a little. At the end of 1987, he visited Washington and was named Man of the Year by *Time* magazine. Two months later he announced that the Soviet Union would withdraw from Afghanistan. The communist government staggered on for several years under constant attack by the Mujahedin until, in 1996, the capital city of Kabul was seized by the Taliban, a political–religious group spawned by the Mujahedin.[20]

The Middle East was the setting for some of the more nefarious Cold War clandestine activities perpetrated by the West. The USA, for example, was not the first country to go to war on a pretext, as it did in Vietnam. Britain and France did just that when they attacked Egypt at the time of Suez. The overthrow of Mossadeq in Iran is an early example of the West attempting to overthrow a country's ruler through the use of clandestine operations. It is not surprising, therefore, that distrust was proba-bly the most significant element of the relationship between

Middle Eastern countries and the Cold War powers. For Middle Eastern leaders, it was a case of a pox on both their houses. As a result, the region provides a good example of the transitory nature of allegiances during the Cold War. Whereas in some regions of the world such as Asia alliances were more firmly rooted in shared ideology or interests, the friendship of a Middle Eastern country was superficial, not something to be relied upon. Egypt, Iraq and Iran were pro-British at the end of the Second World War but soon changed their tune as rulers came and went and the fight for control of oil reserves intensified. After Suez, Egypt turned towards the Russians. Iraq's anti-American stance changed to one of friendship during the Iran–Iraq War whereas Iran's pro-Western policy was transformed into bitter hostility towards the USA after the Iranian Revolution. Islamism, the new political theology of the age, was an enemy of both communism and capitalism. Its strength was in large measure the product of attempts to repel the interventionism of both the USA and the USSR.

The powerful weapon of many Middle Eastern countries was oil. The presence of this natural resource coloured the attitudes of both East and West towards these volatile potential allies and strengthened the hand of Middle Eastern rulers. By comparison, the leaders of African states, most of them newly come to international politics, were on the whole less fortunate. Those countries rich in natural resources that attracted the attention of the Cold War powers, such as the Belgian Congo, did so only to their detriment.

9
Africa

Two momentous power struggles took place in Africa during the second half of the twentieth century. The one was a part of the global conflict between communism and capitalism; the other was between African nationalism and white supremacy. Across the world, the collapse of colonial empires was caught up in the power struggle between East and West, but the manner in which the nationalist struggle in Africa became entangled with the Cold War was peculiar to that continent. In Asia and the Middle East, the throwing off of the colonial yoke frequently led to the re-emergence of countries which had previously had their own distinct identities. In Africa, it was not uncommon for the leaders of new nation states to be working on a blank canvas. National borders were not the result of centuries of history but of colonial rulers drawing lines on maps. As a result, the struggle for identity in Africa was more complex, often tribal and open to greater manipulation.

At the start of the Cold War, almost the whole of the huge African land mass was under the control of Western European countries. The two major colonial powers were Britain and France. British colonies were concentrated in eastern and southern Africa while the French were dominant in northern and western regions. In terms of the Cold War conflict, the two other colonial powers of note were Belgium and Portugal. Belgium ruled a large central area known as the Belgian Congo (renamed Zaire from 1971 to 1997, now the Democratic Republic of Congo [DRC]). Portugal occupied Angola and Mozambique, lying on the western and eastern southern coasts respectively. Only two countries, Ethiopia and Liberia, had never been explicitly colonised but both were firmly in the American sphere of influence.

From the late 1950s, and responding to pressure from Washington, both Britain and France made some preparation for independence in their respective colonies by establishing the trappings of autonomy – constitutions, bureaucracies, legislatures, and educational, judicial and military systems. The French, in particular, saw it as their mission to create independent African states in their own image and, as a rule, retained their influence in their former colonies. When the former British and French colonies became independent, the administrative gap was filled by systems that had had at least a little time to bed in and these countries remained relatively stable during the Cold War. By contrast, the Portuguese, who had been entrenched in Angola since the seventeenth century, refused to contemplate the idea of independence until they were forced to do so by rebellion and civil war. The Belgians adopted a similar attitude.

Neither the USA nor the Soviet Union had a history of direct involvement in Africa and neither showed much interest in the continent until the middle years of the Cold War. America had been content to leave Africa to the Europeans. Russian imperial ambitions, whether of the Tsars or of the commissars, had focused on territory closer to home. However, as the African independence movement gathered pace, fears grew in Washington that African hostility to former colonialists could provide opportunities for communists to step into any vacuum that was left. Many new African leaders leaned towards socialism and looked to the Russians and others for assistance. They were also not averse to playing the two superpowers off against each other. In reality, the economic weakness of the Russians and problems in Europe and Asia prevented them from offering much help to Africa other than in the diplomatic arena.

Nevertheless, both superpowers and their acolytes were keen to take advantage of political vacuums. As a rule, the relationship that developed between the superpowers and infant African states was mutually parasitic. African leaders used the Cold War ideological struggle to obtain what they needed for their own purposes, some more astutely than others, while the West and the Soviet bloc sought to establish political power bases and protect or secure access to the riches of Africa's raw material resources. Major Cold War confrontations occurred in the early 1960s in central Africa, in the mid-1970s in southern Africa, and periodically in the Horn of Africa as Ethiopia and Somalia, both strategically important because of their proximity to the Middle East, oscillated between American and Soviet support.

China also stepped onto the African stage after Zhou Enlai, the Chinese Prime Minister, made a lengthy tour of the continent in 1964 at a time when African nationalism was at a high point. Subsequently, Chinese aid was also on the shopping list of the leaders of Africa's new nations. One of the first countries to feel the impact of Chinese African policy was the tiny island state of Zanzibar. Dominated by Arab and British influences, the independence history of this speck in the Indian Ocean is a microcosm of the African Cold War story. While Britain and America looked on anxiously, teetering on the brink of intervention, Zanzibar was wooed by at least five communist countries. It was an illustration of the manner in which the world's major political players squabbled over every morsel that fell from the African table of independence. The Americans reported that the Russians, Chinese and East Germans descended on Zanzibar 'like the Three Kings, bearing gifts of economic and military aid and opening embassies'.[1] Communist comrades vied for influence with each other. Stasi spymaster Markus Wolf recorded that a portrait of Ulbricht was rapidly replaced by that of Mao Zedong in Zanzibarian offices once the Chinese arrived. The British position was that the situation could best be controlled through the neighbouring President of Tanganyika, Julius Nyerere. They were proved right. The union of Zanzibar with its much larger neighbour took place while the island's pro-Chinese foreign minister was out of the country and succeeded in 'smothering Zanzibar's revolutionary embers in its embrace'.[2]

One of the more surprising facts about the Cold War in Africa is that the struggle between capitalism and communism on that continent was as often as not spearheaded on the communist side by the Caribbean island of Cuba rather than by the monolithic Soviet Union. It was Cuba which sent soldiers, equipment and aid workers to Angola, Mozambique and Guinea-Bissau during the 1970s and to Algeria and several other countries at other times. By 1988, for example, there were 52,000 Cuban soldiers in Angola. The traffic was not all one way. About 40,000 Africans were funded to study at Cuban universities.[3] The Russians were of course active, especially in Angola and Ethiopia, as were the East Germans and the Czechs. But it was Cuba which caused the greatest headaches for the former colonialists of the West and their superpower ally, the USA.

The wave of independence in Africa swept through the continent from north to south throughout the 1950s, 1960s and 1970s. The transition was initially precipitated by the Suez crisis in 1956, its impact being felt first in neighbouring North African states. The first black African country to become independent was the British colony of the Gold Coast (now Ghana) in 1957. Its leader, Kwame Nkrumah, distanced himself from Britain and established himself as a pan-African figurehead, a model to which others aspired, the 'torchbearer' of black Africa.[4] Other British colonies which became independent during the 1960s included Nigeria, Sierra Leone, Tanganyika (later Tanzania), Uganda and Kenya.

It was Guinea that became the first sub-Saharan French colony to celebrate its independence in 1958, establishing a form of socialism and severing its ties with France. The French reacted by stripping the country of 'virtually the entire machinery of government' and halting all forms of investment and assistance.[5] Elsewhere, France managed to keep its former colonies within its sphere of influence. Mali, Niger, Mauritania, Senegal, Burkina Faso, Benin, Cote d'Ivoire, Chad, Gabon, Togo, the Central African Republic and Congo Brazzaville all became independent in this manner in 1960 and, with the French retaining their grip, there were few long-lasting points of tension with the occasional exception of Chad.

This was in sharp contrast to the other major country which achieved independence during this period – the Belgian Congo. The first major Cold War conflict in sub-Saharan Africa erupted in the former Belgian colony during the early 1960s. It proved to be a bloody, brutal and deeply conspiratorial struggle. Thousands were killed, both black and white, the elected Prime Minister was murdered, and Dag Hammarskjöld, the Secretary-General of the United Nations, lost his life in a suspicious plane crash while on a peacekeeping mission. The Congo was the first of several terrible examples of the Cold War in action in Africa.

Crisis in the Congo

The Congo had been colonised by the Belgians in the nineteenth century and had been treated as a personal treasure trove by their king, Leopold II. A huge country in the centre of Africa, it was rich in copper, uranium, diamonds and other resources. During the first half of the twentieth century, the Congo ceased to be the personal fiefdom of the Belgian monarch and passed under the control of the Belgian government, which administered the Congo from afar with the assistance of the Catholic Church and big mining companies. The Belgians made no attempt to build up a black educated elite and there were no more than 30 Congolese university graduates in the whole country at the time of independence and almost no one with any experience of administration at a senior level. Thus it was that when, in 1960, there were violent clashes as the Belgians came under pressure to grant the colony independence, there was no government in waiting. When the Belgians suddenly and rapidly withdrew, the result was anarchy.

The Congo story has many facets, the most clearly cut of which is that elections were held in which a young nationalist firebrand, Patrice Lumumba, won enough votes to form a coalition government and was installed as Prime Minister. Joseph Kasavubu, the leader of a tribal political party and a rival of Lumumba, was named as a figurehead President. Within a matter of days the army, still under the command of Belgian officers, had mutinied, demanding higher pay and better conditions. Deciding that the army should be run by the Congolese, Lumumba chose a junior officer, Joseph Mobutu, as chief of staff. The violence, however, intensified, and the Belgians, uninvited, flew in military reinforcements to try and control the situation and protect their citizens. Lumumba then declared that the Congo was at war with Belgium.[6]

Shortly afterwards, taking advantage of the chaos and with Belgian support, the mineral-rich province of Katanga seceded, forming a separate state under the leadership of a local politician and sworn enemy of Lumumba, Moise Tshombe. Katanga's mines were owned and operated by Belgian companies and many Belgian citizens were caught up in the fierce fighting that took place. Lumumba called upon the UN to help him expel the Belgian soldiers who, he claimed, were attempting to recolonise the Congo. The UN responded by sending troops but was not prepared to take military action to force the Belgian soldiers to leave.

Lumumba then turned to the Soviet Union for help. The Russians provided planes, trucks and a small number of military advisors.[7] This action confirmed American fears that Lumumba was an 'African Castro' and the decision was taken to mount a covert operation to oust him.[8] The Americans gave their backing to Kasavubu who dismissed Lumumba, although it is debatable whether he had the authority to do so. Lumumba was placed under house arrest under the apparent protection of the UN. Meanwhile, Mobutu, who was also backed by the West, announced that he was taking power and ordered the expulsion of all Soviet bloc personnel. Despite UN protection, Lumumba was captured by Mobutu and taken to Katanga where he was tortured and handed over to Tshombe and, in January 1961, shot by firing squad under the command of a Belgian officer.[9]

Despite Lumumba's death, his influence remained strong. In many parts of Africa as well as the Soviet Union and Cuba, he was regarded as a martyr in the struggle against colonialism and the rule of mercenaries. Lumumba's murder did not bring peace or stability to the Congo. Fierce fighting continued between pro-Lumumba and government forces. White mercenaries, many funded and equipped by the USA, were recruited to quell anti-government rebels. In 1964, the Russians, who had largely stood on the sidelines of what was to them a power struggle between tribes and individuals, intervened on the side of the pro-Lumumba rebels. Like the USA, however, it was not prepared to become directly involved in the conflict. The only non-African country to do that was Cuba which sent a handful of soldiers, led by the revolutionary leader Che Guevara, to support the pro-Lumumba rebels.[10] Conflict continued in the Congo until 1965 when Mobutu declared himself President and remained so until 1997, with the consistent backing of the USA. In 2001, following a parliamentary enquiry, Belgium admitted that some former Belgian ministers bore 'some moral responsibility' for the assassination of Lumumba but did not link the Belgian government directly to the killing.[11]

Hammarskjöld and fifteen other UN staff died in an air crash on the Northern Rhodesian–Katangan border on 17 September 1961, while on the way to broker a ceasefire in the region. Foul play was suspected. There were allegations that the plane had been shot down. Possible suspects included white mercenaries, Belgian mining interests and Tshombe forces, and both British and US involvement was suspected. There had been a delay of several hours in searching for the crashed plane, without which there may have been survivors. A UN enquiry into the crash in 1962 found that the cause could not be explained. Sabotage could not be excluded but neither was there any evidence for it. Pilot error was the preferred explanation.

The complexity of the back story reveals a world even murkier than that of African tribal rivalries and former colonial ambitions. The deaths of Lumumba and Hammarskjöld illustrate not just the calculated brutality of the conflict but also the degree of involvement of the numerous different interest groups. The questions continue: questions such as who was responsible for Lumumba's death; what was the role of the UN in the Congo and how did Hammarskjöld, who was deeply and personally involved in the whole Congo affair, meet his death; and what was the extent of US involvement in the Congo crisis and the violent conflicts which took place?

The issue of Lumumba's murder was addressed to a certain extent by the Americans themselves during a 1975 US Senate investigation into 'Alleged Assassination Plots Involving Foreign Leaders' by the Church Committee. One of the murders under investigation was that of Lumumba. In a brief explanation of US covert activity, the committee reported that it regarded the 'unfortunate events' under investigation as 'an aberration, explainable at least in part, but not justified, by the pressures of the time. The Congo, freed from Belgian rule, occupied the strategic center of the African continent, and the prospect of Communist penetration there was viewed as a threat to

American interests in emerging African nations.'[12] CIA cables were presented to the enquiry as evidence. In one of them, CIA chief Allen Dulles, wrote:

> In high quarters here it is the clear-cut conclusion that if (Lumumba) continues to hold high office the inevitable result will at best be chaos and at worst pave the way to communist takeover of the Congo with disastrous consequences for the prestige of the UN and for the interests of the free world generally. Consequently we conclude that his removal must be an urgent and prime objective and that under existing conditions this should be a high priority of our covert action.[13]

Although the enquiry concluded that the USA was not responsible for Lumumba's death, it was not for want of trying. CIA agents had been ordered to kill him. A poison which reproduced a disease indigenous to that part of Africa was sent to the Congo from the USA for that purpose in the autumn of 1960.[14] It was stressed repeatedly that it must not be possible to trace Lumumba's death back to the USA in any way. It proved difficult to obtain access to Lumumba and administer the poison (one plan was to put it on his toothpaste), and there was also talk of shooting him with a hunting rifle. The enquiry also reported a second plan to try and draw Lumumba out of the UN's protective custody so that he could be captured by rival Congolese forces and killed by them. This indeed happened although the enquiry found no 'evidentiary basis' for concluding that the CIA conspired in the actual events which resulted in Lumumba's death.

Lumumba was essentially a nationalist rather than a communist, but his request for Soviet assistance in bringing order to the Congo led the Americans to place him squarely in the Russian camp, despite the fact that there is some evidence to suggest that Washington was aware of his true political affiliations.

'Lumumba is an opportunist and not a communist. His final decision as to which camp he will eventually belong will not be made by him but rather will be imposed upon him by the outside,' read one diplomatic cable from the Congo to Washington in July 1960.[15] But, in American eyes, even if Lumumba was not a communist, his 'erratic behaviour' made him a target for communist subversion.[16] Washington was haunted by the idea that the Congo could become an African Cuba. Another cable from the Congo read: 'Whether or not Lumumba actually commie or just playing commie game to assist his solidifying power, anti-West forces rapidly increasing power Congo and there may be little time left in which to take action avoid another Cuba.'[17] It was the US ambassador in the Congo who urged Lumumba to call in the UN and to exclude the major powers from the force assembled thinking that this would help to keep the Russians out. He told Washington after the UN force had been activated: 'This should keep bears out of the Congo caviar.'[18]

The UN peacekeeping force, one of the largest in its history, was unduly influenced by the Americans. The USA provided about forty per cent of its total funding. In addition, recent research indicates that Hammarskjöld and some of his colleagues secretly collaborated with US officials, an allegation made by the Russians at the time.[19] The Hammarskjöld story, however, rumbles on, with Conor Cruise O'Brien, a UN representative in the Congo at the time and later a member of the Irish government, alleging sabotage in a newspaper letter in 1992.[20] More recently, it has been claimed that the plane crashed after Belgian agents working to split Katanga from the Congo forced it down.[21]

Following the Congo affair, Africa moved down the agenda of both superpowers. The USA was preoccupied with the war in Vietnam. The Russians were keeping a wary eye on their Chinese rivals. In addition, a general reduction in tension resulting from the move towards détente also had its impact in Africa. It was events in Portugal which suddenly put Africa firmly back on the Cold War map.

Civil war in Angola

The catalyst for this major Cold War conflict was the domestic Portuguese coup of 1974 in which the right-wing dictator, Marcello Caetano, was ousted by left-wing army officers. Following a transitional period, this led to democracy being established in Portugal. During the early 1960s, the right-wing Portuguese government had resisted demands for independence in its African colonies of Angola, Mozambique and Portuguese Guinea. This intransigence had led to fierce and sustained guerrilla warfare in these colonies, not only against Portuguese forces but also between rival groups of independence fighters, some backed by the Soviet bloc and others backed by the West. The conflict had sapped the Portuguese army and economy and was a major factor in bringing about the 1974 Lisbon coup. The new Portuguese government belatedly introduced a policy of decolonisation.

Angola became independent in November 1975, having been riven by a liberation war since 1961. The rush to independence after the Lisbon coup merely increased the ferocity of the fighting between the different independence movements: the People's Movement for the Liberation of Angola (MPLA) backed by the communists; the National Union for the Total Independence of Angola (UNITA), backed by the USA and South Africa; and the National Front for the Liberation of Angola (FNLA), backed by non-left groups in southern Africa. America, Russia, Cuba and South Africa were all involved.

The socialist government of Portugal had handed power to

the Marxist MPLA on independence. As in the Belgian Congo, however, the Americans did not relish the idea that communism would take a hold in this strategically important part of Africa. Only Namibia separated Angola from the white supremacy regime of South Africa, which was itself struggling to retain its grip on Namibia despite UN and international opposition. South Africa was the most economically powerful country in Africa and presented itself as a bastion against communism. As such, it was an important ally of the West, despite the difficulties these countries experienced at home in justifying support for the apartheid regime. After the debacle of Vietnam, the USA was reluctant to be drawn into more wars in foreign parts. However, its fear of a domino effect in southern Africa if Angola should turn communist ensured that it did not remain on the sidelines. Kissinger worried that a failure to 'counter Moscow's moves' in Angola could lead the world to question America's resolve.[22] The USA determined to fight communism in Angola by proxy and covertly.

In October 1975, the civil war became an international conflict when South Africa, with the covert support of the USA, invaded Angola. Cuban forces entered the fray as the South Africans advanced towards the Angolan capital of Luanda. Their presence was sufficient to force the South Africans to retreat. The fact that it was Cuba rather than the Soviet Union which was the main supporter of the MPLA in Angola is a story that has only recently been fully recognised.[23]

The MPLA and the Cubans prevented the South Africans from taking the capital, and the MPLA consolidated itself as the governing party in Angola. The West professed itself to be disturbed by South Africa's military intervention in Angola and voiced its criticism. US involvement remained hidden and recent research indicates that America washed its hands of the operation, much to the fury of South Africa. P. W. Botha, the South African President, fulminated later:

I know of only one occasion in recent years when we crossed a border, and that was in the case of Angola when we did so with the approval and knowledge of the Americans. But they left us in the lurch. We are going to retell the story: the story must be told of how we, with their knowledge, went in there and operated in Angola with their knowledge, how they encouraged us to act and, when we had nearly reached the climax, we were ruthlessly left in the lurch.[24]

UNITA, supported by the South African army and American weaponry continued its guerrilla war against the MPLA for the next decade but US covert assistance came to an end when the American Senate blocked funds for such activities. Turbulence continued throughout the area until the end of the 1980s when the UN brokered a peace agreement between the rival groups and oversaw the withdrawal of foreign troops.

Conflict in the Horn of Africa

A region of Africa which was particularly susceptible to Cold War rivalry was the Horn of Africa, that area bordering the Red Sea composed of Ethiopia, Eritrea, Djibouti and Somalia. There was much that divided the countries of the Horn but they shared the fact that they were strategically important, being situated close to the Suez Canal at a point where the Middle East rubs shoulders with Africa. They also bridged the gap between the Middle East and sub-Saharan Africa and had religious and cultural ties with both the Arab world and black Africa. The hostilities which occurred in this region were brought about by a history of territorial disputes plus the ability of rival leaders to equip themselves with massive military hardware thanks to the benefi-cence of their Cold War godfathers. It was in the Horn that the Soviet Union made its most significant African intervention.

The major conflict in the area centred on Somalia's determination to incorporate the whole of what it claimed to be its territory within its borders. The country was poor and backward. Different parts of it had been colonised by Italy, Britain, France and its neighbour Ethiopia. The British and Italian parts of Somalia achieved independence in 1960 but the French refused to hand over Djibouti and the Ethiopians continued to occupy the Ogaden Desert. Both these areas were claimed by Somalia which focused its attacks on Ethiopia, a weaker adversary than France. Ethiopia, ruled at the start of the Cold War by Emperor Haile Selassie, was unlike other African countries. It had a long independent history and its elite was predominantly Christian. With the rise of Islamism, Ethiopia's Christian traditions ensured that the regional and Cold War conflict in the Horn also became one of Islam against Christianity.

Selassie was an important Western ally. The USA was not prepared to leave the defence of the region to the French, who had a military base in Djibouti, especially since the former British colony of South Yemen just across the water from Somalia, declared itself to be the People's Democratic Republic of Yemen in 1967 and opened the door to Soviet advisers. Washington set about forming an alliance with Ethiopia's ruler. The Somalis looked to Russia for support. Somalia's tactics included encouraging small tribal liberation movements within Ethiopia's borders. It also placed itself more squarely in the Soviet camp by becoming a socialist republic in 1969. Thanks to Russia and America, there was a huge military build-up in the area.

In 1974, Selassie was deposed in a coup. The new ruler, Mengistu Haile Mariam, was a Marxist. He determined to rid himself of previous ties with the Americans and set about modernising the country along a path of revolutionary socialism. Washington at first chose to support Mengistu seeing Ethiopia as a vital US toehold in the region. But President Carter, with his emphasis on human rights, found it increasingly hard to square his ethical policy with the brutality of the regime. In any case, Mengistu by 1977 was looking to Russia for support thus seeming to bring all the countries around the southern end of the Red Sea into the Soviet orbit.

But regional ambitions and feuds again took precedence over Cold War allegiances. Somalia, still intent on expanding its borders at Ethiopia's expense, attacked Ethiopia in the Ogaden Desert in 1977 and Russia and other Soviet bloc countries including Cuba went to the aid of their new ally, Ethiopia. After initial victory, Somali forces were driven back and Somalia, turning to Washington for help, found a willing if covert supporter. The conflict continued into the 1980s with a peace agreement being signed between Ethiopia and Somalia in 1988. The leaders of both countries were victims of the end of the Cold War. President Barre of Somalia fled in January 1991 and died in Nigeria in 1995. Mengistu was deposed in 1991 and fled to Zimbabwe.

The conflict between Ethiopia and Somalia was fed by the Cold War and its legacy continues to be felt. During the last twenty years, there has been a settling of old East–West scores resulting in fierce fighting and anarchy. Ethiopia, the former Soviet stronghold, has become a US ally against Islamic forces in Washington's former Cold War ally, Somalia.

The story of the Cold War in Africa is largely the story of anti-colonialism. In the early years, the conflict was between the old European imperial powers and African colonies fighting for independence. In the later years the struggle changed to one of opposition to the new imperialists, the USA and the Soviet Union. Washington feared the power vacuum left by the departure of the Europeans and hastened to fill the gap heedless of the fact that this frequently entailed supporting repressive and corrupt regimes. African leaders seized their opportunities when they could, exploiting the rivalry between the two superpowers and, in later years, between Russia and China. One of the effects of the Cold War in Africa was that there was a massive build-up of military power within a number of different states, this power frequently being turned against civilian rulers. The growth of the armed forces was to the detriment of democracy and human rights, military coups becoming commonplace. As one expert on African affairs has commented, 'a particularly malign effect of the Cold War in Africa was the uncritical support by the West, for blindly strategic reasons, to some highly undemocratic African governments. This has had the knock-on effect of a long delay in democratisation in some instances, the explosion of new wars in others (such as Rwanda, Congo, Liberia, Sierra Leone, Sudan) and the almost complete failure of the most fragile states (with Somalia the extreme but not the only example).'[25]

With the end of the Cold War, most of the continent of Africa has reverted to being of marginal interest within the context of international affairs.

Conclusion: echoes of the Cold War

The twentieth-century struggle between communism and capitalism continues to shape the world we live in. Most visible is the legacy of instability and unfinished business which the Cold War left across the globe. The ideological struggle wrapped its tentacles around places far removed from its European centre and is directly related to events in countries such as Afghanistan, the two Koreas and Somalia during the last twenty years. As the protests of the new non-communist Russia to encroachment from the West have become ever louder, the cry has been heard as to whether the world has entered a new Cold War. In reality, it is more plausible that current conflicts are an extension of the old Cold War, the past two decades or so having been merely an interlude.

The world did not start with a clean slate when the Berlin Wall fell. For a start, the West's belief that it had a mission to export democracy to the rest of the world did not die with the collapse of communism. Old attitudes and prejudices are difficult to expunge. Just as Germany continued to be seen as the enemy for many years after the end of the Second World War, so there is a popular tendency to regard the new Russia as an enemy despite the fact that the country is a member of international forums such as the G8 (Group of Eight) and a vital supplier of energy to Europe.

And so, the Cold War echoes around us. As the USA prepares its missile bases in Poland despite Russian protests, the mind turns to Cuba and the missile crisis of 1962. Will the Russians feel the need to use similar tactics to rid themselves of a perceived threat as they did during the Cuban crisis when threatened by American missiles along the Russo-Turkish border? As former members of the Soviet empire flex their muscles apparently in the name of independence and democracy, what insights can be gained from an understanding of the realities of Cold War revolts in Soviet bloc countries? What is the connection between the uprisings in the GDR, Poland, Hungary and Czechoslovakia during the Cold War, fomented by the USA in such a manner as to make them appear spontaneous, and more recent unrest in places such as Ukraine and Georgia, backed by the West, which has resulted in pro-Western leaders being appointed? Is it reasonable to assume that in the decades between the 1950s, say, and the present day, the CIA's tactics of nourishing resistance without compromising its spontaneous nature have been forgotten or deemed to be unacceptable? That seems unlikely. As NATO creeps towards Russia's borders, is the Kremlin's reaction comparable to American overreaction to the threat of communism in Latin America, an area it considered to be its own backyard, and can Russian actions therefore be justified? Can the Russians use the same arguments to justify their military intervention in Georgia in 2008 as the Americans did when they invaded Guatemala in 1954; or Grenada in 1983; or, indeed, Cuba in 1961? What does the fabrication of evidence in order to justify an attack on Vietnam in 1964 teach us about the evidence collected in order to justify an attack on Iraq in 2003? Perhaps, most significantly, the principle of territorial integrity evaporated during the Cold War, and has not been reinstated. Interference in the affairs of another country is commonplace. NSC 68 justified the use of force in other countries during the Cold War in order to defend American beliefs and principles. Do these principles remain in operation?

There are other echoes which are of a lesser intensity but serve to remind us of the extent to which the world under the Bush regime reverted to the use of antagonistic rhetoric rivalling that of the Cold War. Kennedy's message of tolerance and co-operation, delivered in 1963, was drowned out once again in the post-Cold War age. His call for Americans to examine their own attitudes, not just those of their perceived enemies, his warning that suspicion breeds suspicion, has been largely unheeded. Then there is Carter's speech in which he told the American people that they had been 'too willing to adopt the flawed and erroneous principles and tactics of our adversaries, sometimes abandoning our own values for theirs. We've fought fire with fire, never thinking that fire is better quenched with water.' These words have resonance at a time when the USA and Britain stand accused of abandoning human rights in the interests of fighting the so-called War on Terror. When George W. Bush spoke of the 'axis of evil' in 2002 he was merely echoing Reagan's description of the communist world as an 'evil empire'. The rhetoric of the Cold War was transported almost verbatim to the War on Terror.

The influence of the Cold War can also be seen in the manner in which international relations and, indeed, the internal affairs of nations are handled. The means by which the Cold War was conducted — proxy regional wars, covert operations and propaganda — have remained the tools of governments. They can be seen at work in the new global conflict between religious fundamentalism and democracy — as the Cold War mores of capitalism are more usually marketed in the changed circumstances of the twenty-first century.

The existence of covert operations and intelligence agencies has become a part of everyday life, referred to on a regular basis in the media. This is a major development from the days when the very existence of organisations such as MI6 was denied. Governments have worked at developing more sophisticated methods of presenting their arguments to a less trusting public. Their success can be judged by the fact that public recognition of Cold War manipulation of attitudes and events remains low. As has been seen in this book, events that are overt – that is to say wars and revolutions which are visible to all – are only a part of the picture. The covert aspect relates to the manner in which these events are presented to domestic or non-aligned audiences, and in the organisation of clandestine operations intended to create situations which governments can use to justify their policies. These methods of operation spring directly from the Cold War, examples from that period being evident during the Suez Crisis, the Vietnam War and the invasion of Grenada.

But perhaps the greatest long-term transformation in the affairs of the world, and also the least recognised, is that the concept of human rights has been firmly embedded within international relations, and the moral certitude that protection of these rights justifies intervention in the domestic affairs of other states is accepted by many without question. This is the end result of the process which began in Helsinki in 1975 and is arguably the most significant legacy of the Cold War. It is a major philosophical and political development which remains to be more fully explored and evaluated. The manner in which the West used the issue of human rights as a tool with which to defeat communism is, as yet, largely unknown or ignored. Indeed, so tightly are the people of the former non-communist world gripped by the mission to bring human rights to all that they frequently fail, in biblical terms, to examine the mote in their own eye. In this global rush for human rights for all, the concept of historical evolution or respect for different cultural traditions is often overlooked.

It is, of course, not surprising that the aftershocks of the Cold War continue to reverberate around the world. The twentieth century was a period of huge international turmoil. The Cold War was a major part of that turmoil and arose, in part, from the wars and revolutions which preceded it. In a similar manner, the Cold War continues to shape the twenty-first century. Where the Cold War differs from most previous conflicts is that its ending was not marked by major international peace treaties and therefore its ending was less defined. The unfinished business continues.

Chronology

1945 (August)	Nuclear age begins when the USA drops an atomic bomb on Hiroshima, Japan
1945 (September)	Vietnam declares independence under Ho Chi Minh
1947 (March)	Truman Doctrine pledges to support 'free people' resisting subjugation
1947 (June)	Marshall Plan introduced
1948 (March)–1949 (May)	Berlin Blockade
1949 (April)	NATO created
1949 (May)	West Germany created
1949 (1 October)	The Chinese People's Republic created under Mao Zedong
1949 (7 October)	German Democratic Republic created
1950–1953	Korean War
1953 (March)	Death of Stalin
1953 (June)	Uprising in East Berlin
1953 (August)	Mohammed Mossadeq overthrown in Iran following a covert operation by the USA and Britain, probably the first example of a regime change operation in the Cold War
1954 (May)	French defeated in Vietnam at Dien Bien Phu
1954 (June)	Jacobo Arbenz deposed in

	Guatemala with CIA assistance, the first US covert intervention in Latin America
1954 (July)	Geneva Agreements end French involvement in Indo-China and Vietnam divided into North and South
1954 (November)	Start of the Algerian War of Independence
1956 (June)	Uprising in Poland
1956 (October)	Uprising in Hungary
1956 (October)	Suez crisis
1957 (January)	Eisenhower Doctrine marks the entry of the USA into Middle Eastern affairs
1957 (March)	First black African colony (Ghana, formerly the Gold Coast) obtains independence
1958 (January)	Start of the Great Leap Forward in China
1958 (July)	Iraqi Revolution and the start of the rise of the Baath Party
1960 (July)	Congo Crisis
1961 (January)	Patrice Lumumba, Prime Minister of the Congo Republic, murdered
1961 (April)	Bay of Pigs invasion of Cuba by US-backed exiles
1961 (August)	Berlin Wall erected
1962 (October)	Cuban Missile Crisis
1963 (June)	Kennedy makes keynote speech aimed at reducing Cold War tensions
1963 (July)	The policy of East–West co-operation, Ostpolitik, is made

	public by politician Egon Bahr in a speech in West Germany
1963 (November)	Kennedy assassinated
1964 (October)	Khrushchev deposed
1965 (April)	US troops intervene in civil war in the Dominican Republic
1965–1968	Cultural Revolution in China
1965–1973	Vietnam War
1968 (April)	Prague Spring
1968 (August)	Formulation of the Brezhnev Doctrine giving Soviet bloc countries the right to intervene in other countries if communism was threatened
1968 (August)	Czechoslovakian Uprising and invasion by Warsaw Pact countries
1969 (January)	Nixon becomes US President
1969 (March)	Russian and Chinese troops clash on China's northern border
1969 (November)	Start of the SALT negotiations
1970 (August)	West Germany recognises GDR borders
1972 (February)	Nixon visits China
1972 (May)	Signing of SALT 1
1973 (January)	Vietnam War ends with signing of peace agreement in Paris
1973 (September)	Salvador Allende overthrown in Chile in a military coup backed by the USA and replaced by Augusto Pinochet
1975 (July)	Helsinki Accords
1975 (November)	Angola granted independence.
1976 (April)	The united Socialist Republic of Vietnam declared

1977 (January)	Carter becomes US President
1978 (October)	Election of the Polish Cardinal Karol Wojtyla as Pope John Paul II
1979 (February)	Iranian Revolution and establishment of the Islamic Republic under Khomeini
1979 (June)	Pope visits Poland
1979 (November)	Iranian hostage crisis
1979 (December)	Russia sends troops into Afghanistan, start of the Afghan War
1980 (August)	Birth of Solidarity in Poland
1980 (September)	Start of Iraq–Iran War
1981 (January)	Reagan becomes US President
1981 (December)	Martial law declared in Poland
1983 (March)	Reagan's 'evil empire' speech
1983 (October)	US invasion of Grenada
1984 (May)	Russia pulls out of Los Angeles Olympic Games
1985 (March)	Gorbachev becomes Soviet leader
1986 (November)	Iran-Contra Affair revealed
1989 (October)	Hungarian Communist Party reformed as a social democratic party
1989 (November)	Opening of the Berlin Wall
1989 (December)	Velvet revolution in Czechoslovakia
1990 (December)	Lech Wałęsa becomes President of Poland

Notes

Introduction

1 Aldrich, *Hidden Hand*, p. 1.

Chapter 1

1 See Brendon, *The Dark Valley*, for an engrossing account of the turbulent world which preceded the Cold War.

2 Karl Marx and Friedrich Engels, *Manifesto of the Communist Party*. There have been numerous publications of this small book over the past hundred years in many languages. The most commonly printed English language version is the 1888 translation by Samuel Moore. Usually this also contains a number of prefaces by Engels. The work is also frequently published under the title of *The Communist Manifesto*.

3 Kolakowski, *Main Currents of Marxism*. This book was chosen as one of the hundred most influential books since the war by the Central and East European Publishing Project, the list being published in the *Bulletin of the American Academy of Arts and Sciences*, 1996.

4 Ibid., p. 533.

5 See Wheen, *Karl Marx* for a very readable account of Marx's life and work.

6 See, for example, the 'Statement' made by the West German politician, Egon Bahr, recorded in the *Bulletin of the German Historical Institute*, Supplement 1, 2004, p. 142: 'the factor of ideological collapse has been underestimated [in assessing the reasons for the collapse of the Soviet bloc] ... the dissolution of the ideological cement that kept the whole thing together was surely a central factor ... It is quite possible that, if the ideological structure had been firm, there would have been an explosion with an ensuing massacre rather than an implosion.'

7 Marx, *Manifesto*.

8 Kolakowski, *Main Currents of Marxism*, p. 1.

9 Marx, *Manifesto*.

10 Ibid.

11 Jeffrey Kopstein, 'Ulbricht Embattled: The Quest for Socialist Modernity in the Light of New Sources', *Europe–Asia Studies*, 46, 4, 1994, pp. 597–615.

12 Pipes, *Communism: A Brief History*, Ch. VI.

13 Marx, *Manifesto*.

14 Weber, *The Protestant Ethic and the Spirit of Capitalism*, first published in 1904.

15 Schumpeter, *Capitalism, Socialism and Democracy*, first published in 1942.

16 Larry Diamond and Marc F. Plattner (eds), *Capitalism, Socialism, and Democracy Revisited*, first published in the *Journal of Democracy*, 1992.

17 Frieden, *Global Capitalism*, p. xvi.

18 Ibid., pp. 475–476.

19 See Barber, *Consumed*, for a critique of twenty-first century capitalism.

20 Barber, 'Invisible hand has to be led by us all', *The Times Higher Education Supplement*, 25 May 2007.

21 Ibid.

Chapter 2

1 John Lewis Gaddis, *We Now Know: Rethinking Cold War History*. See also Gaddis, 'On Starting All over Again: A Naïve Approach to the Study of the Cold War' in *Reviewing the Cold War*.

2 Aldrich, *The Hidden Hand*, pp. 5–7.

3 Philby, *My Silent War*, first published in 1968; B. Page, D. Leitch and P. Knightley, *Philby*.

4 Wolf with McElvoy, *Man Without a Face*, Ch. 9; Michael Frayn, *Democracy*.

5 Amy Knight, 'Annual Report of the KGB to Leonid Brezhnev on its Operations for 1967', *CWIHP Bulletin*, 10, 1998, p. 218.

6 Harry S. Truman, speech to the American Society of Newspaper Authors, 20 April 1950, quoted by Hixson, *Parting the Curtain*, p. 14.

7 The CIA ran both Radio Free Europe targeted at the Soviet Union, and Radio Liberty aimed at Soviet bloc countries.

8 Quoted by Hixson, *Parting the Curtain*, p. 13.

9 Quoted by Saunders, *Who Paid the Piper?*, p. 1.

10 Carl Bernstein, 'The CIA and the Media', *Rolling Stone*, 20 October 1977.

11 Quoted by W. Scott Lucas and C. J. Morris in 'A Very British Crusade: the Information Research Department and the Beginning of the Cold War' in *British Intelligence Strategy and the Cold War*.

12 Scott Lucas, Letter to the Editor, *Independent*, 26 February 1995. See also Lucas and Morris, 'A Very British Crusade'.

13 Quoted by Buckow, *Zwischen Propaganda und Realpolitik*, p. 578.

14 Aldrich, *The Hidden Hand*, p. 11.

15 For detailed accounts of CIA activities in Western Europe see Saunders, *Who Paid the Piper?*; Trevor Barnes, 'The Secret Cold War: The CIA and American Foreign Policy in Europe 1946–1956', *The Historical Journal*, 24, 1981, pp. 399–415 and 25, 1982, pp. 649–670; Aldrich, *The Hidden Hand*.

16 Andrew and Mitrokhin, *The Mitrokhin Archive*, p. 462.

17 Aldrich, *The Hidden Hand*, pp. 5–7.

18 Andrew and Mitrokhin, *The Mitrokhin Archive* and *The Mitrokhin Archive II*.

19 Quoted by Beatrice Heuser, 'Covert Action within British and American Concepts of Containment, 1948–1951', in *British Intelligence Strategy*.

20 The CWIHP is at http://www.wilsoncenter.org/index.cfm?fuseaction=topics.home&topic_id=1409. It is based at the Woodrow Wilson International Center for Scholars in Washington DC and focuses on new findings from the former communist world. The National Security Archive (NSA) is available at http://www.gwu.edu/~nsarchiv/index.html. It is an independent

non-governmental research institute and library located at The George Washington University, USA. It collects and publishes declassified documents obtained through the US Freedom of Information Act.

21 See, for example, a CIA report about its dealings with the Soviet double agent Oleg Penkovsky run jointly by the CIA and MI6, 22 October 1966.

22 See Vladimir Pozniakov, 'A NKVD/NKGB Report to Stalin: A Glimpse into Soviet Intelligence in the United States in the 1940s', *CWIHP Bulletin*, 10, 1998, p. 220.

23 Quoted by Sir Michael Quinlan, Permanent Under-Secretary of State at the Ministry of Defence from 1988 to 1992, in his introduction to *Cabinets and the Bomb*.

24 A range of views on these questions can be found in *Cold War Statesmen Confront the Bomb*.

25 For more on nuclear history see the National Security Archive Electronic Briefing Books on Nuclear History at http://www.gwu. edu/~nsarchiv/NSAEBB/#Nuclear%20History; Hughes-Wilson, *The Cold War*, particularly 'Appendix: How the Cold War was Fought'; Mastny, Holtsmark and Wenger (eds), *War Plans and Alliances*.

Chapter 3

1 Examples include British and Soviet actions during the Warsaw Uprising in 1944, see Irina Mukhina, 'New Revelations from the Former Soviet Archives: The Kremlin, the Warsaw Uprising, and the Coming of the Cold War' in *Cold War History*, 6, 3, 2006, pp. 397–411; and the destruction of Dresden in a firestorm in 1945, see Frederick Taylor, *Dresden: Tuesday 13 February 1945* (London: Bloomsbury, 2004).

2 Marc Trachtenberg, 'The Myth of Potsdam' in *Haunted by History*.

3 Future Policy Study Committee Memoranda, 1959–1960, Macmillan Cabinet Papers 1957–1963, NA, CAB 134/1929, p. 56. Available online from Adam Matthews Publications.

4 Sean Greenwood, 'Bevin, the Ruhr and the Division of Germany: August 1945–December 1946', *The Historical Journal*, 29, 1, 1986, pp. 203–212.

5 Winston Churchill, speech at Westminster College, Fulton, Missouri, 5 March 1946.

6 Loth, *Stalin's Unwanted Child*.

7 Truman's speech to a joint session of the US Congress, 12 March 1947.

8 Dianne Kirby, 'Divinely Sanctioned: the Anglo–American Cold War Alliance and the Defence of Western Civilisation and Christianity, 1945–1948', *Journal of Contemporary History*, 35, 3, pp. 385–412.

9 Bryson, *The Life and Times of the Thunderbolt Kid*, p. 187.

10 Quoted by Saunders, *Who Paid the Piper?* p. 191.

11 William Stivers, 'The Incomplete Blockade: Soviet Zone Supply of West Berlin, 1948–1949', *Diplomatic History*, 21, 4, 1997, pp. 569–602.

12 Truman Papers, 'Memorandum for the President. The Situation in Germany, July 23 1948'.

13 Christian Ostermann, 'The United States, the East German Uprising of 1953, and the Limits of Rollback', CWIHP Working Paper No. 11, December 1994.

14 Mark Kramer, 'The Early Post-Stalin Succession Struggle and Upheavals in East-Central Europe: Internal-External Linkages in Soviet Policy Making. Part 3', *Journal of Cold War Studies*, 1, 3, 1999, pp. 3–66.

15 Ostermann, 'The United States, the East German Uprising of 1953', CWIHP Working Paper No. 11.

16 Ibid.

17 Ibid.

18 Izabella Main, 'National and Religious Holidays as the Clashing Point of the State, the Church and Opposition in Poland, 1944–1989' (Ph.D diss., Central European University, Budapest, Hungary, 2002), Ch. 3.

19 Johanna Granville, '"Caught with Jam on Our Fingers": Radio

Free Europe and the Hungarian Revolution of 1956', *Diplomatic History*, 29, 5, 2005 pp. 811–839.

20 Corey Ross, 'East Germans and the Berlin Wall: Popular Opinion and Social Change before and after the Border Closure of August 1961', *Journal of Contemporary History*, 39, 1, 2004, pp. 25–43.

21 Stasi Archives, BStU, MfS HAXX/4/357, anonymous report on Frau Seigewasser, December 1960.

22 Brandt, *People and Politics*, p. 20.

23 Raymond Garthoff, 'Berlin 1961: The Record Corrected', *Foreign Policy*, 84, 1991, pp. 142–156.

24 SAPMO–BArch NY 182/1317 GDR government archives, report on a meeting with Crossman in East Berlin, 11 August 1961.

Chapter 4

1 Geraint Hughes, 'British Policy towards Eastern Europe and the Impact of the "Prague Spring", 1964–68', *Cold War History*, 4, 2, 2004, pp. 115–139.

2 Future Policy Study, 1960.

3 Frank Cain, review of 'Spies Beneath Berlin', *Journal of Intelligence History*, 3, 2, 2003.

4 *Izvestia*, 23 November 1973, quoted by British diplomat Bryan Cartledge in a report on détente and the ideological struggle, NA FCO 28/2564.

5 *Pravda*, 22 August 1973, Cartledge as above.

6 Brezhnev speech, 15 August 1973.

7 John F. Kennedy, commencement address at the American University, Washington DC, 10 June 1963, John F. Kennedy Presidential Library and Museum.

8 *The Times*, 15 June 1963.

9 Brandt, *People and Politics*.

10 See Thomas, *Communing with the Enemy*, Ch. 3.

11 Bahr, *Bulletin of the German Historical Institute*, Washington DC, Supplement 1, 2004.

12 Brezhnev, speech to Polish communists, 13 November 1968.

13 Hughes, 'British Policy towards Eastern Europe'.

14 Vojtech Mastny, 'Was 1968 a Strategic Watershed of the Cold War?', *Diplomatic History*, 29, 1, 2005, pp. 149–177.

15 Stasi Archive, BStU, MfS HA XX/4/3233, report on Czechoslovakia, 20 May 1968.

16 Thomas, *Communing with the Enemy*.

17 Stasi Archive, BStU, MfS AP 21497/92, report on Müller-Gangloff, 21 February 1964.

18 NA PREM 11/4583, meeting between Harold Macmillan, Dean Rusk and others in London, 24 June 1962, *Macmillan Cabinet Papers*.

19 Bahr, *Bulletin of the German Historical Institute*.

Chapter 5

1 NA, CAB 195/9, Cabinet Secretaries' Notebooks, Cabinet meeting, 12 April 1951.

2 Carter, commencement speech, Notre Dame University, 22 May 1977.

3 Zbigniew Brzezinski, *The New Dimensions of Human Rights*, Fourteenth Morgenthau Memorial Lecture on Ethics and Foreign Policy, Carnegie Council on Ethics and International Affairs, 1995.

4 CIA, RP 77–10100D, The Soviet View of the Dissident Problem Since Helsinki, 1 May 1977.

5 Ibid.

6 Ibid.

7 Main, 'National and Religious Holidays'.

8 FCO, ENP 226/1, report of the British Embassy in Warsaw to the British Foreign Secretary on the Pope's visit to Poland, 2 May 1979.

9 Main.

10 FCO, ENP 226/1, British Foreign Office report on the Pope's visit to Poland, 13 July 1979.

11 Ibid.

12 FCO, ENP 226/1, British Foreign Office report on the Pope's visit to Poland, 24 July 1979.

13 Garton Ash, *The Polish Revolution*, p. 73.

14 *The Times*, 25 October 1980.

15 Loth, 'Moscow, Prague and Warsaw: Overcoming the Brezhnev Doctrine', *Cold War History*, 1, 2, 2001, pp. 103–118.

16 Garton Ash, *The Polish Revolution*, p. 121.

17 CIA, RP 77–10100D.

18 Matthew Ouimet, 'National Interest and the Question of Soviet Intervention in Poland, 1980–1981: Interpreting the Collapse of the Brezhnev Doctrine', *Slavonic and East European Review [Great Britain]*, 78, 4, 2000, pp. 710–734.

19 CIA, F-1993–01602, Gorbachev biography, 1 August 1985.

20 Barbara Farnham, 'Reagan and the Gorbachev Revolution: Perceiving the End of the Threat', *Political Science Quarterly*, 116, 2, 2001, pp. 225–252.

21 O'Dochartaigh, *Germany Since 1945*, p. 185.

Chapter 6

1 Hennessy, *Having It So Good: Britain in the Fifties* (London: Penguin, 2007), p. 133.

2 *The Times*, 9 February 1966. The film was *The War Game*, directed by Peter Watkins. It was eventually screened in 1985.

3 Marina Oborotova, 'Russian Policy in Latin America: Past, Present and Future', *Latin American Research Review*, 28, 3, 1993, pp. 183–188.

4 See Munton and Welch, *The Cuban Missile Crisis*, for a detailed but concise account of the crisis. Also Gott, *Cuba*, Ch. 6.

5 R. F. Kennedy, *13 Days*. The film *Thirteen Days* was directed by Ronald Donaldson and starred Kevin Costner.

6 Gott, *Cuba*, p. 195.

7 Fursenko and Naftali, '*One Hell of a Gamble';* Fursenko and Naftali, *Khrushchev's Cold War*.

8 NSA, Electronic Briefing Book, *Kennedy and Castro: the Secret History*, 'Kennedy Sought Dialogue with Cuba', 2003.

9 Hughes-Wilson, *The Cold War*, p. 197.

10 See Westad, *The Global Cold War*, Ch. 4, and the CIA website, http://www.foia.gov

11 Jorge I. Domínguez, 'US–Latin American Relations During the Cold War and Its Aftermath', *The United States and Latin America*, Bulmer-Thomas and Dunkerley, eds.

12 Westad, *The Global Cold War*, p. 201.

13 For more on this subject see Jerome Slater, 'The Domino Theory and International Politics: the Case of Vietnam', *Security Studies*, 3, 2, December 1993, pp.186–224.

14 NSA, Electronic Briefing Book 110, Peter Kornbluh, *Nixon on Chile Intervention*, 2004.

15 Haslam, *The Nixon Administration and the Death of Allende's Chile*.

16 Domínguez.

17 Hughes-Wilson, *The Cold War*, p. 259.

18 *The Times*, 25 April 1983.

19 NSA, Electronic Briefing Book 210, Malcolm Byrne, Peter Kornbluh and Thomas Blanton, *The Iran–Contra Affair 20 Years On 1983–1988*, 2006.

20 Westad, *The Global Cold War*, p. 345.

21 *The Times*, 21 October 1983.

22 *The Times*, 29 October 1983, letter from Kenneth Walker.

23 Oborotova.

Chapter 7

1 Westad, *The Global Cold War*, p. 187.

2 Westad, *The Global Cold War*, pp. 160–170 for more on the Sino–Soviet split.

3 Future Policy Study, 1960.

4 Shen Zhihua, 'Sino–Soviet Relations and the Origins of the Korean War: Stalin's Strategic Goals in the Far East', *Journal of Cold War Studies*, 2, 2, 2000, pp. 44–68.

5 Stephen Casey, 'Selling NSC-68: The Truman Administration, Public Opinion, and the Politics of Mobilization, 1950–51', *Diplomatic History*, 29, 4, 2005, pp. 655–690.

6 Peter Lowe, 'Change and Stability in Eastern Asia: Nationalism, Communism and British Policy, 1948–1955', *Diplomacy and Statecraft*, 15, 2004, pp. 137–147.

7 Hughes-Wilson, *The Cold War*, p. 98.

8 One of the major online booksellers, for example, lists 2839 entries under the Vietnam War history category compared with 652 for the Korean War.

9 Nina Tannenwald, 'Nuclear Weapons and the Vietnam War', *Journal of Strategic Studies*, 29, 4, pp. 675–722.

10 See record of an online discussion between American historians entitled 'Legacies of the Vietnam War', *Journal of American History*, 93, 2, 2006, pp. 452–490.

11 Church Committee. Also NSA, Electronic Briefing Book, John Prados, *JFK and the Diem Coup*, 2003.

12 *The Times*, 22 December 1969.

13 Moïse, *Tonkin Gulf*; Hughes-Wilson, *The Cold War*, p. 215; National Security Agency website http://www.nsa.gov/vietnam/index.cfm

14 Foley, *Confronting the War Machine*.

15 David L. Anderson, 'One Vietnam War Should Be Enough and Other Reflections on Diplomatic History and the Making of Foreign Policy', presidential address to the Society for Historians of American Foreign Relations (SHAFR), *Diplomatic History*, 30, 1, 2006, pp. 1–21.

16 Ibid., p. 12.

17 Ibid., p. 19.

18 Antonio Vasori, 'Britain and US Involvement in the Vietnam War during the Kennedy Administration, 1961–1963', *Cold War History*, 3, 2, 2003, pp. 83–112.

19 Westad, *The Global Cold War*, Ch. 5.

20 Chen Jian, 'China's Involvement in the Vietnam War, 1964–69', *The China Quarterly*, 142, 1995, pp. 356–387.

Chapter 8

1 Fred Halliday, 'The Middle East, the Great Powers, and the Cold War', *The Cold War and the Middle East*, p. 14.

2 Sayigh and Shlaim (eds), *The Cold War and the Middle East*.

3 Andeed Dawisha, 'Egypt', *The Cold War and the Middle East*, p. 29.

4 David Tal, 'Weapons without Influence: British Arms Supply Policy and the Egyptian–Czech Arms Deal, 1945–55', *The Journal of Imperial and Commonwealth History*, 34, 3, 2006, pp. 369–388.

5 Baath in Arabic means 'renaissance'. See Polk, *Understanding Iraq*, p. 107. For a description of the Syrian origins of the party, see Westad, *The Global Cold War*, p. 123.

6 Charles Tripp, 'Iraq', *The Cold War and the Middle East*, Ch. 8.

7 Polk, *Understanding Iraq*, p. 115.

8 Reports from the British Embassy in Baghdad to the Foreign Office, British reference FCO 17/871, contained in *The Saddam Hussein Sourcebook* posted online by the NSA http://www.gwu.edu/~nsarchiv/special/iraq/index.htm

9 NSA, Memorandum of Conversation, Henry Kissinger *et al.* with Iraqi Minister of Foreign Affairs Sa'dun Hammadi, 17 December 1975.

10 NSA, Donald Wilber, Summary to 'Overthrow of Premier Mossadeq of Iran, November 1952–August 1953', Electronic Briefing Book 28, *The Secret CIA History of the Iran Coup, 1953*. Also see Gasiorowski and Byrne (eds), *Mohammad Mossadeq and the 1953 Coup in Iran*.

11 Westad, *The Global Cold War*, pp. 295–296.

12 NSA, Joyce Battle (ed.), *Shaking Hands with Saddam Hussein: The U.S. Tilts toward Iraq, 1980–1984*, Electronic Briefing Book 82, 2003.

13 Ibid., secret Department of State report on the meeting between Rumsfeld and Saddam, 20 December 1983.

14 Joe Stork, 'US Involvement in Afghanistan', *Middle East Research and Information Project Reports*, 89, 1980, pp. 25–26. Amin had studied at Columbia University in New York.

15 NSA, Steve Galster, 'Afghanistan: The Making of US Policy, 1973–1990', *The September 11th Sourcebooks Volume II: Afghanistan: Lessons from the Last War*, 2001, John Prados and Svetlana Savranskaya (eds).

16 Westad, *The Global Cold War*, p. 319.

17 NSA, Galster, *Afghanistan*.

18 Hughes-Wilson, *The Cold War*, p. 280; Stork, 'US Involvement in Afghanistan'.
19 NSA, Galster, *Afghanistan*.
20 Westad, *The Global* Cold *War*, Ch. 10, for more on the Taliban government.

Chapter 9

1 Gleijeses, *Conflicting Missions*, p. 60.
2 Ibid.
3 Piero Gleijeses, 'Moscow's Proxy: Cuba and Africa 1975–1988', *Journal of Cold War Studies*, 8, 2, 2006, pp. 3–51.
4 Veen, *What Went Wrong With Africa*, p. 22.
5 Ibid., p. 35.
6 Meredith, *The State of Africa*, Ch. 6.
7 David N. Gibbs, 'The United Nations, International Peacekeeping and the Question of "Impartiality": Revisiting the Congo Operation of 1960', *Journal of Modern African Studies*, 38, 3, 2000, pp. 359–382.
8 Gleijeses, *Conflicting Missions*, p. 61.
9 Meredith, *The State of Africa*, p. 112.
10 Gleijeses, *Conflicting Missions*, p. 89.
11 Meredith, *The State of Africa*, p. 114.
12 Interim Report of the Church Committee.
13 Allen Dulles, cable to station officer, 26 August 1960, Interim Report of the Church Committee.
14 The plot to poison Lumumba was confirmed in documents released by the CIA in 2007. See http://www.gwu.edu/~nsarchiv/NSAEBB/NSAEBB222/index.htm
15 Kalb, *The Congo Cables*, p. 36.
16 Schraeder, *United States Foreign Policy toward Africa*, p. 55.
17 Ibid., p. 56.
18 Kalb, p. 7.
19 David N. Gibbs, 'Secrecy and International Relations', *Journal of Peace Research*, 32, 2, 1995, pp. 213–228.

20 Bengt Rosio, 'The Ndola Crash and the Death of Dag Hammarskjöld', *The Journal of Modern African Studies*, 1993, pp. 661–671.
21 Matthew Hughes, 'The Man Who Killed Hammarskjöld', *London Review of Books*, 23, 15, 9 August 2001.
22 Clough, *Free at Last?*, p. 10.
23 See Gleijeses, *Conflicting Missions*.
24 Quoted by Gleijeses in 'Moscow's Proxy?', *Journal of Cold War Studies*.
25 Richard Synge, Senior Editor, *The Africa Report*.

Bibliography

Africa

Michael Clough, *Free at Last? US Policy Towards Africa and the End of the Cold War* (New York: Council on Foreign Relations Press, 1992).

Piero Gleijeses, *Conflicting Missions: Havana, Washington and Africa, 1959–1976* (Chapel Hill and London: University of North Carolina Press, 2002).

Madeleine G. Kalb, *The Congo Cables: The Cold War in Africa – from Eisenhower to Kennedy* (New York: Macmillan, 1982).

Martin Meredith, *The State of Africa: A History of Fifty Years of Independence* (London: Simon & Schuster, 2006).

Peter J. Schraeder, *United States Foreign Policy toward Africa: Incrementalism, Crisis and Change* (Cambridge: Cambridge University Press, 1994).

Roel van der Veen, *What Went Wrong With Africa* (Amsterdam: KIT Publishers, 2004).

Asia

Michael S. Foley, *Confronting the War Machine: Draft Resistance During the Vietnam War* (Chapel Hill: University of North Carolina Press, 2003).

Roderick MacFarquhar and Michael Schoenhals, *Mao's Last Revolution*, (Cambridge MA: Belknap Press, 2006).

Robert J. McMahon, *The Limits of Empire: the United States and Southeast Asia since World War II* (New York: Columbia University Press, 1999).

Robert S. McNamara, James G. Blight, Robert K. Brigham; with

Thomas J. Biersteker and Herbert Y. Schandler, *Argument without End: In Search of Answers to the Vietnam Tragedy* (New York: Public Affairs, 1999).

Edwin E. Moïse, *Tonkin Gulf and the Escalation of the War in Vietnam* (Chapel Hill: University of North Carolina Press, 1996).

Marilyn B. Young and Robert Buzzanco, eds, *A Companion to the Vietnam War* (Oxford: Blackwell, 2006).

Qiang Zhai, *China and the Vietnam Wars, 1950–1975* (Chapel Hill: University of North Carolina Press, 2000).

Communism and capitalism

Benjamin Barber, *Consumed: How Markets Corrupt Children, Infantilize Adults, and Swallow Citizens Whole* (New York and London: Norton, 2007).

Larry Diamond and Marc F. Plattner, eds, *Capitalism, Socialism, and Democracy Revisited* (Baltimore and London: Johns Hopkins University Press, 1993).

Jeffry A. Frieden, *Global Capitalism: Its Fall and Rise in the Twentieth Century* (New York and London: Norton, 2006).

Leszek Kolakowski, *Main Currents of Marxism: Its Rise, Growth, and Dissolution*, trans. P. S. Falla (Oxford: Clarendon Press, 1978).

Karl Marx and Friedrich Engels, *Manifesto of the Communist Party.*

Richard Pipes, *Communism: A Brief History* (London: Weidenfeld and Nicolson, 2001).

Joseph Schumpeter, *Capitalism, Socialism and Democracy* (London: Unwin, 1987).

Max Weber, *The Protestant Ethic and the Spirit of Capitalism*, trans. Talcott Parsons with an introduction by Anthony Giddens (London and New York: Routledge Classics, 2001).

Eastern Europe

Timothy Garton Ash, *The Polish Revolution: Solidarity* (London: Penguin, 1999).

Robin Okey, *The Demise of Communist East Europe* (London: Arnold, 2004).

Mark Pittaway, *Eastern Europe 1939–2000* (London: Arnold, 2004).

General Cold War

Michael L. Dockrill and Michael F. Hopkins, *The Cold War, 1945–1991* (Basingstoke: Palgrave Macmillan, second edition 2006).

Saki Ruth Dockrill, *The End of the Cold War Era: The Transformation of the Global Security Order* (London: Hodder Education, 2005).

John Lewis Gaddis, *We Now Know: Rethinking Cold War History* (Oxford: Clarendon, 1997).

John Hughes-Wilson, *The Cold War: the Hidden Truth about how Close We Came to Nuclear Conflict* (London: Robinson, 2006).

Martin Leffler, *For the Soul of Mankind: The United States, the Soviet Union, and the Cold War* (New York: Hill & Wang, 2007).

Jeremy Smith, *The Fall of Communism* (Basingstoke: Palgrave Macmillan, 2005).

Odd Arne Westad, *The Global Cold War: Third World Interventions and the Making of our Times* (Cambridge: Cambridge University Press, 2007).

Odd Arne Westad, ed., *Reviewing the Cold War: Approaches, Interpretations, Theory* (London and Portland: Frank Cass, 2000).

Germany

Willy Brandt, *People and Politics: the Years 1960–1975*, trans. J. Maxwell Brownjohn (London: Collins, 1978).

Anjana Buckow, *Zwischen Propaganda und Realpolitik: die USA und der sowjetisch besetzte Teil Deutschland 1945–1955* (Stuttgart: Franz Steiner, 2003).

Wilfried Loth, *Stalin's Unwanted Child : the Soviet Union, the German Question and the Founding of the GDR*, trans. Robert F. Hogg (Basingstoke: Macmillan, 1998).

Pól O'Dochartaigh, *Germany Since 1945* (Basingstoke: Palgrave Macmillan, 2004).

Merrilyn Thomas, *Communing with the Enemy: Covert Operations, Christianity and Cold War Politics in Britain and the GDR* (Oxford and Bern: Peter Lang, 2005).

Intelligence

Richard J. Aldrich, *The Hidden Hand: Britain, America and Cold War Secret Intelligence* (London: John Murray, 2002).

Richard J. Aldrich, ed., *British Intelligence Strategy and the Cold War, 1945–1951* (London: Routledge, 1992).

Christopher Andrew and Vasili Mitrokhin, *The Mitrokhin Archive: the KGB in Europe and the West* (London: Allen Lane, 1999).

Christopher Andrew and Vasili Mitrokhin, *The Mitrokhin Archive II: the KGB and the World* (London: Allen Lane, 2005).

Walter L. Hixson, *Parting the Curtain: Propaganda, Culture and the Cold War, 1945–1961* (London: Macmillan, 1997).

Bruce Page, David Leitch and Phillip Knightley, *Philby: The Spy Who Betrayed a Generation* (London: André Deutsch, 1968).

Kim Philby, *My Silent War* (London: Grafton, 1989).

Frances Stonor Saunders, *Who Paid the Piper? the CIA and the Cultural Cold War* (London: Granta, 2000).

David Stafford, *Spies Beneath Berlin* (London: John Murray, 2002).

Markus Wolf with Anne McElvoy, *Man Without a Face: the Memoirs of a Spymaster* (London: Jonathan Cape, 1997).

Latin America and the Caribbean

Victor Bulmer-Thomas and James Dunkerley, eds, *The United States and Latin America: The New Agenda* (London: Institute of Latin American Studies, University of London, 1999).

Aleksandr Fursenko and Timothy Naftali, *'One Hell of a Gamble': Khrushchev, Castro, Kennedy and the Cuban Missile Crisis 1958–1964* (London: John Murray, 1997).

Richard Gott, *Cuba: A New History* (New Haven and London: Yale University Press, 2005).

Jonathan Haslam, *The Nixon Administration and the Death of Allende's Chile: A Case of Assisted Suicide* (London: Verso Press, 2005).

Robert F. Kennedy, *13 Days: the Cuban Missile Crisis* (London: Macmillan, 1969).

Alan McPherson, *Intimate Ties, Bitter Struggles: The United States and Latin America since 1945* (Washington DC: Potomac, 2006).

Don Munton and David A. Welch, *The Cuban Missile Crisis: A Concise History* (New York and Oxford, Oxford University Press, 2007).

Middle East

Mark J. Gasiorowski and Malcolm Byrne, eds, *Mohammad Mossadeq and the 1953 Coup in Iran* (Syracuse: Syracuse University Press, 2004).

William R. Polk, *Understanding Iraq: A Whistlestop Tour from Ancient Babylon to Occupied Iraq* (London: I. B. Taurus, 2006).

Yezid Sayigh and Avi Shlaim, eds, *The Cold War and the Middle East* (Oxford: Clarendon Press, 1997).

Military

John Lewis Gaddis, Philip H. Gordon, Ernest R. May and Jonathan Rosenberg, eds, *Cold War Statesmen Confront the Bomb: Nuclear Diplomacy since 1945* (New York: Oxford University Press, 1999).

Peter Hennessy, ed., *Cabinets and the Bomb* (Oxford, Oxford University Press, 2007).

Vojtech Mastny, Sven Holtsmark and Andreas Wenger, eds, *War Plans and Alliances in the Cold War: Threat Perceptions in East and West* (London: Routledge, 2006).

Soviet Union

Aleksandr Fursenko and Timothy Naftali, *Khrushchev's Cold War: The Inside Story of an American Adversary* (New York: W. W. Norton, 2006).

Sergei Khrushchev, ed., *Memoirs of Nikita Khrushchev: Volume I, Commissar, 1918–1945*, trans. George Shriver, supplemental material translated by Stephen Shenfield (Pennsylvania: Pennsylvania State University Press, 2004).

Melvyn Leffler, *For the Soul of Mankind: The United States, the Soviet Union, and the Cold War* (New York: Hill & Wang, 2007).

David R. Marples, *The Collapse of the Soviet Union, 1985–1991* (Harlow: Pearson Education, 2004).

Fiction, biography, drama and miscellaneous

Piers Brendon, *The Dark Valley: A Panorama of the 1930s* (London: Pimlico, 2001).

Bill Bryson, *The Life and Times of the Thunderbolt Kid: Travels through my Childhood* (London: Transworld, 2007).

Cyril Buffet and Beatrice Heuser, eds, *Haunted by History : Myths in International Relations* (Providence, RI and Oxford: Berghahn, 1998).

Michael Frayn, *Democracy* (London: Methuen, 2003).

Barbara Kingsolver, *The Poisonwood Bible* (London: Faber and Faber, 2000).

Arthur Koestler, *Darkness at Noon* (London: Vintage Classics, 2007).

Francis Wheen, *Karl Marx* (London: Fourth Estate, 2000).

Index